THE
Sprinkles
BAKING BOOK

THE
Sprinkles
BAKING BOOK

100 SECRET RECIPES FROM CANDACE'S KITCHEN

Candace Nelson

WITH Adeena Sussman

PHOTOGRAPHS BY Amy Neunsinger

GRAND CENTRAL
Life & Style
NEW YORK · BOSTON

Hachette Book Group supports the right to
free expression and the value of copyright. The
purpose of copyright is to encourage writers
and artists to produce the creative works that
enrich our culture. The scanning, uploading, and
distribution of this book without permission is a
theft of the author's intellectual property. If you
would like permission to use material from the
book (other than for review purposes), please
contact permissions@hbgusa.com. Thank you
for your support of the author's rights.

Grand Central Life & Style
Hachette Book Group
1290 Avenue of the Americas
New York, NY 10104

www.GrandCentralLifeandStyle.com

Printed in the United States of America

Q-MA

First Edition: October 2016
10 9 8 7 6 5 4 3 2 1

Grand Central Life & Style is an imprint of Grand
Central Publishing.
The Grand Central Life & Style name and logo
are trademarks of Hachette Book Group, Inc.

The Hachette Speakers Bureau provides a wide
range of authors for speaking events. To find
out more, go to www.HachetteSpeakersBureau
.com or call (866) 376-6591.

The publisher is not responsible for websites
(or their content) that are not owned by the
publisher.

Library of Congress Cataloging-in-Publication
Data is available upon request.

ISBN 978-1-4555-9257-9 (hardcover edition)
ISBN 978-1-4555-9259-3 (ebook edition)

BOOK AND COVER DESIGN BY SHUBHANI SARKAR
sarkardesignstudio.com

TO CHARLES

Thank you for the sweetest journey a girl could ask for.

I love you.

CONTENTS

EVERYTHING'S COMING UP CUPCAKES!

I've lived all over the world, but no matter where I go, the reaction to a perfectly frosted cupcake, irresistibly crisp cookie, or towering layer cake is a smile. Dessert is universal, a reminder of what's really important, giving us a reason to celebrate the simple joys of family and friends with a bite of delicious indulgence...and that's why I love it. I always get a kick out of telling people I make cupcakes for a living. Whether it's the editor of a national food magazine or a taxi driver, the result is the same: their eyes light up, and they can't wait to share their cupcake opinions with me. Everyone has something to add to the conversation.

Eleven years ago, I set out to create a special place that would allow me to share this happiness with others. Today, more than a decade into the Sprinkles journey, I still marvel at the magical power of a scratch-made dessert and the way it brings people from all different walks of life together in one happy place.

My lifelong love affair with baking began at an early age in my mother's kitchen, where I watched and learned from her every move, eagerly standing by her side awaiting instructions. She welcomed my help, and I was soon cracking eggs, measuring sugar, and passing flour through her dented aluminum hand-cranked flour sifter on its way into the batter.

I would switch on the flimsy oven light, trying to control my excitement long enough to catch that moment when the baking soda worked its magic, causing the batter to puff and rise. The dim lightbulb and hazy tempered glass did not deter me; I'd press my face right up against the oven door, watching, mesmerized, as the batter ballooned into a perfect dome right before my eyes. I could almost taste that first bite into the sweet shelf of frosting, cold and smooth against the soft cake beneath, still slightly warm because I couldn't quite wait.

Part of my childhood was spent living with my family abroad, and during those years baking became a way for me to reconnect with the all-American flavors that spoke to my sense of home. While we were living in Asia, my mom showed me how to whip my first egg white, gently separating the eggs and making sure not to break the yolks or allow any bits of shell to make their way into the bowl. We made meringues and angel food cakes, undeterred by the tropical humidity that turned our crisp, fresh-from-the-oven meringues into sticky mounds. It was my first lesson in the very delicate nature of baking—and a handy excuse to eat them faster.

A batch of ooey-gooey chocolate chip cookies, a pan of fudgy brownies, a sky-high slice of devil's food cake—I loved them for the way they could transport me, with one single bite, across oceans to a place that was happily familiar. My nostalgia wasn't necessarily for a different time, but for a different place. The process—leveling out the sugar in my mom's plastic measuring cups, following a family recipe from a dog-eared recipe card, buttering the Bundt pan, and presenting the finished goods to my family—connected me not only to them, but to an American tradition I dearly loved.

I set out to bring these memories to life when it came

time to open Sprinkles, the world's first cupcake bakery, in 2005. I yearned to share my philosophy that dessert should, and could, be a daily indulgence. I worked to create a welcoming oasis that captured the childlike wonder I've always derived from the ritual of making desserts, but in a way that reflected my own very particular tastes: fresh and modern, not frilly or fussy, with an aesthetic that would appeal to adults and never condescend to children.

With our understated chocolate-brown facade and tiny neon sign, we were so under the radar on opening week that most customers drove right by, calling in for help with directions before they finally found us. Once they did, it was clear that something unique was happening.

A cupcakes-only bakery? What else do you sell? they'd ask. Although it strayed from the everything-for-everyone mentality that defined many American businesses at the time, I was committed to the idea of doing one thing—and doing it very well. Customers immediately connected with Sprinkles. I like to think it's because they loved our thoughtfully edited offerings and pared-down aesthetic, which felt sleek and welcoming at the same time. They'd linger for an extra minute to survey every last cupcake flavor, ask questions about our recipes, or introduce themselves to me or my husband, Charles, who was personally manning the register when he wasn't running out to the bank for change.

We sold out that first day . . . and have pretty much every day since. I think that one of the reasons we do is because we never forget who we are. At its heart, Sprinkles is still a mom-and-pop shop with me and Charles at the helm. Now, with twenty-two locations and counting, we're a growing company, and one that also sells housemade ice cream and crazily delicious cookies. But back then, I was baking every Sprinkles cupcake by hand, often through the night, mixing the batter, filling the cupcake pans, frosting row upon row of cupcakes while carrying on conversations with customers in the front.

It thrills me to see just how many people we have touched with our desserts, and the way our employees interact with our amazing customers every day. It may seem old-fashioned, but greeting regulars by name, knowing their favorite flavors, taking orders over the phone, running boxes out to their cars, sneaking in a little surprise when we can—that's the way we continue to do business every day.

By now there's an entire generation of kids that has grown up on Sprinkles, who can't imagine celebrating their birthdays without a dozen of our cupcakes decorated just the way they like. We're woven into the fabric of communities and families, bringing generations together over cupcakes, cookies, ice cream—and something else that's a little more intangible but equally powerful. We've been part of life-changing experiences; there was the time a guy proposed to his girlfriend with a carefully orchestrated plan involving our staff—and the shiny pink Cupcake ATM outside our Beverly Hills store. In lieu of her regular s'more cupcake, out popped a shiny diamond ring. My favorite part? After she responded with a resounding "YES!" she promptly asked, "Where's my cupcake?"

Still, it is the everyday moments I love best. On a recent trip to our Dallas store, I couldn't help but notice a grandmother and her granddaughter, dressed in a pink tutu, sharing a cupcake on one of the benches outside. Sprinkles has a hand in thousands of moments just like that one every day, something that makes me prouder than almost anything else we do.

That's why I decided to write this baking book. Although we share home-friendly versions of the secret cupcake and cookie recipes from the Sprinkles shops—and some new twists on the favorites—you'll discover a lot more as you flip through the pages. It's filled with new American baking classics that I love and make myself—and I believe you'll reach for again and again. It's a book you can flip through to find the perfect recipe for every occasion, from a holiday cookie swap to a fancy dinner party.

It was also important to me that every last recipe be eminently doable but still special. Most contain ingredients you can easily find at every supermarket and ask for little more than a little love and attention. The techniques are easy, the results exceptional. There may be a seasonal ingredient here and there, but in most cases you'll be able to bake what you want any time of the year.

Most important, I want the process of baking to be fun: something you can do with your kids, your friends, other loved ones, or on a quiet afternoon by yourself, when the rhythm of baking brings a happy smile. Because at the end of the day, life is meant to be sweet.

Enjoy!

CHAPTER 1

PANTRY & EQUIPMENT

Think of this as your baking palette. With these ingredients on hand, you'll have the basics to create many of the desserts in this book. Like all things culinary, the fresher, the better—even things like chocolate, spices, and baking powder have expiration dates. The best way that I've found to ensure fresh ingredients? Bake as often as possible!

THE SPRINKLES BAKING PANTRY

EGGS

All recipes in this book call for **large eggs**; a standard large egg has about 3 tablespoons of liquid inside. If you notice that your eggs look extra large or really small, you may want to increase or decrease accordingly. Try to use fresh eggs; fresher egg whites may take a little longer to whip, but once you do they'll be more stable.

DAIRY PRODUCTS

I almost always use **plain unsalted butter**; that way, I can control the amount of salt I put into my baked goods. Once in a while, when an extra-rich texture is called for, I use **French-style creamery butter**, such as Plugrá, which has a higher butterfat content and less water. It's great for dense, rich recipes like my Fudgy Brownies (page 150). We also use it in all of the cookies in our stores. **Buttermilk** is a natural by-product of butter production, but the type you buy at the store is produced in larger quantities by adding cultures to low-fat milk. Its tangy flavor and thick consistency add a unique texture and taste to many recipes; its acidic content also acts as a leavening agent. Make sure to shake it before you use it, as it tends to separate in the carton or bottle. For a quick buttermilk substitute, combine 1 cup whole milk with 1 tablespoon lemon juice and let sit for 10 to 15 minutes, or whisk together ½ cup plain whole milk yogurt with ½ cup water until smooth.

    Whole milk shows up most often in our recipes, but we also use half-and-half, a 50/50 split of whole milk and heavy cream (to make your own, simply mix equal parts whole milk and heavy cream).

    Heavy cream, a simple indulgence that improves anything it touches, is essential in my dessert repertoire. In the supermarket, you're likely to come across both heavy cream and heavy whipping cream. The difference lies in the fat content: heavy cream contains a slightly higher fat quotient, allowing it to hold peaks longer and add even more richness to desserts.

    Sour cream and crème fraîche are great bakers' tools, helping develop a moist crumb and adding subtle tang to cakes. While both are made by introducing a culture into a high-fat dairy product, sour cream is typically a little looser and has a slightly lower fat content. Crème fraîche is rich, thick, and usually clocks in at about 30 percent fat, adding a luxurious flourish to cakes, toppings—even frostings.

    Cream cheese is at the heart of many of our frostings; its fluffiness and ever-so-slight tanginess add a distinctive touch. We use full-fat, block-style cream cheese—the kind you can find in any supermarket aisle. Avoid spreadable or whipped cream cheese; they often contain additives of varying density, and will yield frostings with a very different consistency.

PEANUT BUTTER

The recipes in this book call for two types of peanut butter: **Natural-style** peanut butter (we use Laura Scudder's brand at Sprinkles) is less smooth and tends to separate in the jar; make sure to stir to reincorporate the oil into the peanut butter before using. **Supermarket-style** peanut butter, such as Jif or Skippy, typically contains more additives, sugar, and salt, and has a creamier texture thanks to hydrogenated oil. Though we don't use it in the shop, I use it in this cookbook when a super-smooth eating experience is a must.

OIL

Some of our cakes and cookies call for **oil** instead of, or in addition to, butter. Oil provides moistness and neutral flavor and—of course—it's dairy-free. You can use vegetable oil, which is really a blend of different oils, or canola oil. If I can, I like to use expeller-pressed oils, which are made with fewer chemicals than oils manufactured by more conventional methods.

A new favorite in my pantry is **coconut oil**. This rich, fragrant oil has become a staple of the dairy-free and vegan dessert kitchen. At room temperature it's still semisolid, the consistency of a thick hand lotion; cold, it hardens into a solid mass that can be scooped with a spoon. Apply a little heat and it melts into liquid. When using coconut oil, be aware that some coconut flavor will remain in the finished dessert; if you don't like that flavor, seek out a version labeled "refined," which has a less pronounced flavor.

SALT

While I'm a fan of kosher salt for savory cooking, my baking salt of choice is **fine sea salt**; it dissolves faster, and you get a more concentrated saltiness per teaspoon. For finishing, I sprinkle flaky British Maldon sea salt or French fleur de sel on top for a final delicate, salty flourish.

SUGAR

Most of our recipes call for **granulated white sugar**, which is made from the evaporated juice of sugarcane. **Superfine sugar** is granulated sugar that's been pulverized into smaller particles. It's often used in meringues, where it adds sweetness without graininess. **Confectioners' sugar** is made from the same base ingredient, but is processed differently and has a small amount of cornstarch or other anticaking agent added. Confectioners' sugar should always be sifted to avoid clumps.

Brown sugar comes in two varieties: light and dark. Both start with granulated white sugar, but their moist consistency comes from the addition of molasses; dark brown has more molasses than light brown, and a deeper, slightly more intense flavor. Store brown sugar in an airtight container. You may find that it hardens as it sits in the cabinet; to soften it, pop a marshmallow or a slice of white bread in the sugar and seal it in a zip-top bag overnight. The sugar will soften up nicely.

Turbinado sugar (often known by the brand name Sugar In The Raw) is coarse, crystal-like, pale-blond sugar that tastes like light brown sugar's more subtle cousin. Named for the cylindrical turbine it's made in, it adds a delightful sugary crunch, and is great to coat cookies before baking or as an added textural element—

especially in crispy, crunchy desserts. **Sanding sugar**, with its large flakes and crystalline appearance, is used to decorate crusts and cookies, where it lends festive sparkle, shine, and sweetness.

FLOUR

All-purpose flour is the standard for our cupcakes, cakes, and cookies. If you've ever wondered what the difference is between flours labeled "**bleached**" and "**unbleached**," it's simple: both are actually bleached! Bleached flour is chemically treated, while unbleached flour ages longer and bleaches naturally. Conventional wisdom dictates that bleached flour yields baked goods that are slightly more tender and fluffier, while unbleached flour provides more structure. I would consider them interchangeable for these purposes.

Whole wheat pastry flour is made from a strain of wheat that's soft, meaning it grinds up extremely fine, making it a great addition when a slightly nutty taste— but tender texture—is desired. Plain **whole wheat flour** is ground from hard winter wheat, from which the tough outer husk and inner kernel haven't been removed. When ground, it has a heartier texture that I love in recipes such as my Peach & Blackberry Galette (page 203).

Cake flour is ground from lower-protein flour, which yields super-light, airy baked goods. It's great when levity is key, as in my Vanilla Yule Log (page 259).

Nut flours are made by grinding nuts very fine; they are protein packed, gluten-free, and indulgent. Once thought of as health foods, they're now appreciated for the virtues they bring to a dessert: toasty flavor, subtle richness, and tenderness.

LEAVENING AGENTS

Baking soda and baking powder may appear in more of my recipes than any other ingredients, save sugar and flour. They take baked goods to new heights by reacting with acid, heat, or moisture to generate carbon dioxide, giving lift to cakes and cookies.

Baking soda is pure bicarbonate of soda; in large quantities, it can have a slightly metallic taste, and it's powerful stuff, about three times stronger than baking

powder. Recipes calling for baking soda typically contain an acidic component like lemon juice or buttermilk—even molasses or brown sugar—that helps it rise.

Baking powder also contains a base of bicarbonate of soda, but it's cut with cornstarch. Baking powder gets activated two ways: by moisture when it's stirred into a batter, and then again by heat when it hits the oven.

Though these are shelf-stable products, they can lose their potency. To test them, all you have to do is drop a bit of baking powder into hot water, or hot water and vinegar if you are testing baking soda. Look for a bubbling reaction—if there's fizzing, it's still good to use!

COCOA

There's a lot of talk about cocoa powder: to use Dutch process or not? **Dutched** cocoa means it's been alkalized to bring it to a neutral pH (acidity level) of 7. So-called **natural** cocoa hasn't been neutralized, meaning it has a higher pH. The general rule is: for recipes that call for

baking soda, such as my Red Velvet Cupcakes (page 14), use natural cocoa powder; for chocolate recipes that call for baking powder, use Dutched. That being said, I've found that the two types can be used interchangeably with good results.

CHOCOLATE

Obviously, there's a lot of chocolate in this book! At Sprinkles, we've used top-quality chocolate since day one, working with companies like Callebaut, Valrhona, and Tcho, all known for their unwavering quality and purity. Chocolate contains two base components: cacao liquor (also known as cacao paste) and cocoa butter, which both occur naturally in cocoa beans. **White chocolate** (used, for example, in the ganache for our Cocoa Mint Brownies, page 159) is made from cocoa butter, but mixed with no cacao paste. **Dark chocolate** is available in several different varieties distinguishable by their cacao content, the most common being **semisweet** (which can

SPICES

Many of my recipes call for spices, especially so-called warm spices like cinnamon, nutmeg, and ginger. Like all the ingredients in my kitchen, I make sure that my spices are fresh, preferably less than six months old. I was happy to see that McCormick recently started putting expiration dates on their spices—great idea!

EXTRACTS

Except for vanilla, I use flavor extracts very sparingly. Sometimes, as in my Chocolate Peppermint Frosting (page 91) or my Coconut Cupcakes (page 22), however, a little bit can really help reinforce the flavor story of a particular recipe. Remember—err on the side of fewer drops; you can always add more flavor, but you can't take it away!

VANILLA

Many of my recipes call for **vanilla extract**, and this is one area where you don't want to skimp on quality! I recommend Nielsen-Massey Madagascar Bourbon vanilla extract. Made by steeping vanilla beans in an alcohol base, this product is head and shoulders above the rest, lending anything it touches a pure, rich, complex vanilla flavor. Some recipes also call for **whole vanilla beans**, especially in milky recipes like crème brûlée. Though expensive, fresh vanilla beans, with their exquisitely floral flavor, are truly worth the splurge and leave beautiful tiny brown flecks in custard, pudding, and whipped cream. If you can't find vanilla beans, you can swap in 2 teaspoons vanilla extract per vanilla bean.

range from 35 to 61 percent cacao, depending on the brand) and **bittersweet** (typically between 55 and 65 percent cacao). They're swappable in recipes—just know that chocolate labeled "semisweet" has a lower percentage of cacao than bittersweet. Many of my recipes call for chocolate chips—these are not the same as baking chocolate, as they contain stabilizers to help them maintain their shape when baked. Avoid using chocolate chips when the recipe calls for melted chocolate.

BAKING TOOLS & EQUIPMENT

A great set of tools goes a long way to baking success. After spending time in the Sprinkles kitchens for over a decade, I've learned firsthand what works best for every recipe.

CAKE PANS

The key with cake pans, whether round, square, or rectangular, is the material they're made of. Seek out commercial-grade heavyweight aluminized steel, which is superior in terms of durability and heat transfer. USA Pans brand is a great option.

BAKING SHEETS

These come in two versions, rimmed and unrimmed. I opt for rimmed baking sheets because they're the baking industry standard and what I'm most comfortable with. At Sprinkles we use Chicago Metallic brand. Choose substantial, good-quality pans; thin, cheap pans can warp and rust easily.

FINE-MESH STRAINER

This handy piece of equipment does double duty: I push cooked puddings and curds through its tiny holes to eliminate any last lumps, and also use it to tap confectioners' sugar onto desserts for a pretty finishing touch.

COOLING RACKS

These metal racks serve an essential purpose: allowing baked goods to cool by letting air circulate underneath. I like the look and function of grid-patterned racks, which you can find at Sur La Table.

PARCHMENT PAPER

I go through rolls and rolls of this in my kitchen, using it to line pans and create an additional layer of nonstick coating and insulation. Parchment paper also protects bakeware, making for easy cleanup. It comes in bleached versions, which are white, and unbleached versions, which are a natural, kraft-paper brown. I am partial to the unbleached variety, which is sold at Whole Foods and other health and natural foods stores. Buy it in packages of individual sheets or in a tear-off roll.

BLOW TORCH

Also known as a brûlée torch, this butane-powered little gadget almost instantly creates a golden top for crème brûlée or toasty marshmallow-frosted cupcakes. Keep one stashed in your kitchen for those occasions when a fancy flourish is required. Make sure you have an extra can of butane on hand for refills.

PIE PAN

All the pie recipes in this book call for a standard 9-inch pie pan. Metal and ceramic pie pans work really well, but a glass or Pyrex plate is my gold standard for the way it evenly distributes heat and keeps baking "hot spots" to a minimum. Plus, I like the fact that I can see how the bottom crust is browning.

TART PAN

I have these fluted beauties in a variety of sizes. They're great when you're making a dessert with a crust that'll be presented out of its vessel. The removable bottom means you can lift away the sides of the pan; the bottom stays hidden underneath your tart and allows for easy transport to a serving platter.

SPRINGFORM PAN

A high-sided dessert like a cheesecake calls for this ingenious pan, which consists of two pieces: a round bottom and a hinged side piece that clasps around the bottom. After the cake is baked and cooled, the sides can be unclasped and removed, leaving the sides of your dessert exposed. It's a good idea to have both 8- and 9-inch springform pans on hand.

COOKIE CUTTERS

Cookie cutters are so much fun, but the variety can be bewildering. I choose beautiful copper ones for timeless designs (since they're pricier, I call them "investment cutters"), then plastic or stainless steel for novelty shapes. Companies like CopperGifts.com offer a shape for any theme or occasion.

SILICONE SPATULAS

I love good-quality rubber spatulas that can stand up to high temperatures, and I keep a variety of different sizes on hand. The little ones are handy for getting into tight corners and more delicate work, while the larger ones are workhorses for folding egg whites into batter, transferring batter from one vessel to another, and, obviously, mixing! Williams-Sonoma stocks a nice variety of colors and sizes in the heat-resistant, wooden-handled silicone spatulas I am partial to.

WHISKS

Just like rubber spatulas, I buy wire whisks in a variety of sizes. The key is that they are made of sturdy and nonreactive stainless steel for drama-free durability. So-called balloon whisks, with their fuller shape, are great for whisking egg whites and beating cream; slightly narrower French whisks help you get into the corners of a saucepan, making them helpful for making curds and puddings.

CUPCAKE LINERS/BAKING CUPS

Cupcake liners come in a mind-boggling array of options these days. At Sprinkles shops, all our cupcakes live in the same chocolate-brown cupcake wrapper, but at home you can be creative. Wilton standard baking cups in pastel colors can be found in most grocery stores, and Wilton.com is a great online source for cupcake liners. Have fun with colors, but remember that all the cupcake recipes in this book are meant to be baked in a standard-size cupcake liner—no fancy lace-cut or scalloped designs please!

STAND MIXER

I can barely remember a time when I didn't have my trusty KitchenAid mixer. This is the workhorse of my home kitchen—I even outfitted my first Sprinkles kitchen with them before realizing I would need larger, commercial mixers to meet the demands of our hungry customer base. You will never regret an investment in one of these machines. They beat batters and whisk egg whites effortlessly with just the lightest tap of a switch. A handheld mixer can be used in place of a stand mixer, but it will take longer to do the same job.

FOOD PROCESSOR

I use my food processor to puree fruit, make the cookie and graham cracker crumbs that serve as the base for many of my desserts—and always for my master pie dough. In all honesty, I am obsessed with my Breville food processor, which I really do find to be best in class. My Master Pie Crust recipe (page 214), for example, recommends twenty pulses in a standard food processor; in my Breville it comes together beautifully in considerably less than that.

LIQUID AND STAINLESS-STEEL MEASURING CUPS AND SPOONS

In baking, precision is key. So make sure to use cup-style dry measuring cups for dry ingredients like flour and sugar, and liquid measuring cups for liquid ingredients

like oil, water, milk, and cream. Pyrex liquid measuring cups are the industry standard, and it is helpful to have them in both 1- and 2-cup sizes. For dry measuring cups, the key is durability. All-Clad stainless-steel measuring cups and spoons are robust; they've been through the wringer in my kitchen but still look shiny and new.

OVEN THERMOMETER

It's amazing how much home oven temperatures vary. Trust me, if you don't have an oven thermometer hanging inside your oven (most models hook right onto an oven rack), you really don't know if you are baking at 350°F or 315°F, regardless of what your oven dial tells you. For a minor investment of a few dollars, you'll keep your oven honest and save yourself batches of frustration.

CUPCAKE PANS

All the cupcakes at Sprinkles are baked in a Chicago Metallic glazed cupcake pan. You can find them at restaurant supply stores and online. For baking at home, all the cupcake recipes in this book were tested in a standard Wilton 12-cup nonstick cupcake pan (which is actually sold as a "muffin pan"—they're the same thing). The nonstick coating makes the cupcakes release easily, and the pan is simple to clean!

DISHER

At Sprinkles, we scoop cupcake batter with a disher, a spring-release ice cream scoop. This handy device helps us fill the cupcake cups uniformly so all the cupcakes bake at the same rate. I use different-sized dishers depending on the cupcake batter; if you'd like to invest in one for the cupcakes in this book, buy a #16 (¼-cup) disher to feel like a bakery pro!

OFFSET SPATULAS

At Sprinkles, we use an offset spatula to frost our cupcakes, just as I do at home. The recessed angle and "dropped" design of the spatula matches the slight dome of a cupcake perfectly, giving me tons of control and keeping my fingers away from the pristine icing while frosting. You can buy a Sprinkles offset spatula in Sprinkles stores or at Sprinkles.com; otherwise, Ateco brand 4½-inch offset spatulas with either a wooden or black plastic handle are perfect.

CAKE ROUNDS

These disposable corrugated-cardboard circles are a super-convenient way to support and transport cakes. They go under the base of the cake to help you lift it without breakage. And if you plan to give cakes as gifts and don't want to worry about collecting your serving plate later, cake rounds are the way to go. You can buy them in a variety of sizes to match the size of your cake; Wilton makes a whole selection.

CAKE LIFTER

If you don't want to mess with cake rounds, you might at least want to invest in a cake lifter. It's a large round spatula that you slip under a cake and use to transport the cake to your platter or cake stand without breaking it. I particularly like the Nordic Ware cake lifter. It has a 10-inch diameter and is made of thin, sturdy, nonstick metal for safe lifting and smooth release.

CAKE TURNTABLE

I have had my Ateco revolving cake stand (available at Williams-Sonoma stores) for years, and I imagine it will last me forever. With its cast-iron base, it is super sturdy, and the easy-to-maneuver spinning plate allows for 360-degree frosting.

FONDANT CUTTERS AND PLUNGERS

Fondant is a really fun way to customize the decorations on your cupcake or cake. Buy fondant at cake decorating or craft stores (I prefer Satin Ice brand). I like to use Ateco plastic fondant plungers, which can be found at cake decorating or craft stores and come in a variety of shapes, from hearts to snowflakes. After rolling the fondant thin, cut it with the cutter and then use the plunger to pop out the shape.

MIXING BOWLS

I recommend two sets of mixing bowls. First, a set of stainless-steel mixing bowls with a rubber nonskid base that grips the counter to prevent sliding and spares your countertops from scratches. Second, a set of heat-resistant glass mixing bowls, like Pyrex, is crucial in the kitchen. These can be used for melting chocolate in the microwave and can go from there to the freezer and then to the dishwasher without cracking.

BENCH SCRAPER

If you like "working clean" like a pro baker, I recommend this tool, also known as a pastry cutter. Nothing else gathers up excess pie dough on your workspace quite like it, and it's great for cutting dough, too.

CHAPTER 2

EVERYDAY CUPCAKES

This is the chapter where you will find many of the Sprinkles Cupcakes you already know and love, most of which are on regular—if not daily—rotation in our stores. It's such a thrill to be able to share these carefully adapted home versions, which bring the store experience right to your kitchen. Because the cupcake is an innately simple creation, the details count for everything. At my bakeries, we work tirelessly toward perfection: mixing the batter just until the flour is integrated and no more; scooping the exact same amount of batter into each cup so everything bakes at the same rate; spinning the cupcake tray midway through and pulling it from the oven the second the tops are dry; and, finally, frosting the cupcakes the moment they have cooled to seal in freshness.

Each cupcake flavor is scooped in slightly different amounts and has a different baking time; some rise into light cakes while others are denser by design. Each one has a specific personality, and at Sprinkles we know every last quirk. I'm excited for you to get to know each cupcake's characteristics at home, and to make these cupcakes your own.

THE SPRINKLES RED VELVET CUPCAKE

MAKES 12 CUPCAKES OR ONE 2-LAYER 9-INCH CAKE

Two thousand fifteen was a big year for Sprinkles. We celebrated our ten-year anniversary…and more than 25 million red velvet cupcakes sold! And to think, I almost didn't create a red velvet cupcake for Sprinkles. Having grown up in Oklahoma, my husband insisted we add red velvet, his familiar favorite, to the menu. However, most red velvets I'd tried had left me cold. At best, they were made with a teaspoon of cocoa; at worst, they were flavorless lumps altogether devoid of cocoa and distinguished by a shockingly red hue. *All right,* I told Charles, *if I'm going to do red velvet, I'm going to do it my way.* So I upped the cocoa quotient with a luxurious Belgian variety, then colored it a deep burgundy red before topping it with a rich cream cheese frosting. In the early days, many customers came in asking for this mysterious red cupcake with the unfamiliar name—they'd never heard of red velvet! More than a decade later, it has surpassed chocolate and vanilla in popularity. Here, I share the iconic recipe that continues to define Sprinkles to this day.

1½ cups all-purpose flour

3 tablespoons unsweetened cocoa powder

1 teaspoon baking soda

1 teaspoon fine sea salt

⅔ cup buttermilk, shaken

1¾ teaspoons white vinegar

1 teaspoon pure vanilla extract

¾ teaspoon red gel food coloring (see page 17)

10 tablespoons (1¼ sticks) unsalted butter, slightly softened

1 cup plus 2 tablespoons sugar

2 large eggs

Cream Cheese Frosting

Preheat the oven to 350°F. Line a 12-cup cupcake pan with paper liners.

In a medium bowl, whisk together the flour, cocoa powder, baking soda, and salt. In a small bowl, stir together the buttermilk, vinegar, vanilla, and food coloring.

In the bowl of a stand mixer fitted with the paddle attachment, beat the butter and sugar on medium-high speed until light and fluffy, 2 to 3 minutes. Reduce the speed to medium-low, add the

CREAM CHEESE FROSTING

MAKES 2 CUPS

1 (8-ounce) package cream cheese, slightly softened

½ cup (1 stick) unsalted butter, slightly softened

⅛ teaspoon fine sea salt

3¾ cups confectioners' sugar, sifted

½ teaspoon pure vanilla extract

In the bowl of a stand mixer fitted with the paddle attachment, beat the cream cheese, butter, and salt on medium speed until light and fluffy, 2 minutes. Reduce the speed to low, gradually add the confectioners' sugar, and beat until incorporated. Increase the speed to medium, add the vanilla, and beat until fully blended, 1 to 2 minutes, making sure not to incorporate too much air into the frosting.

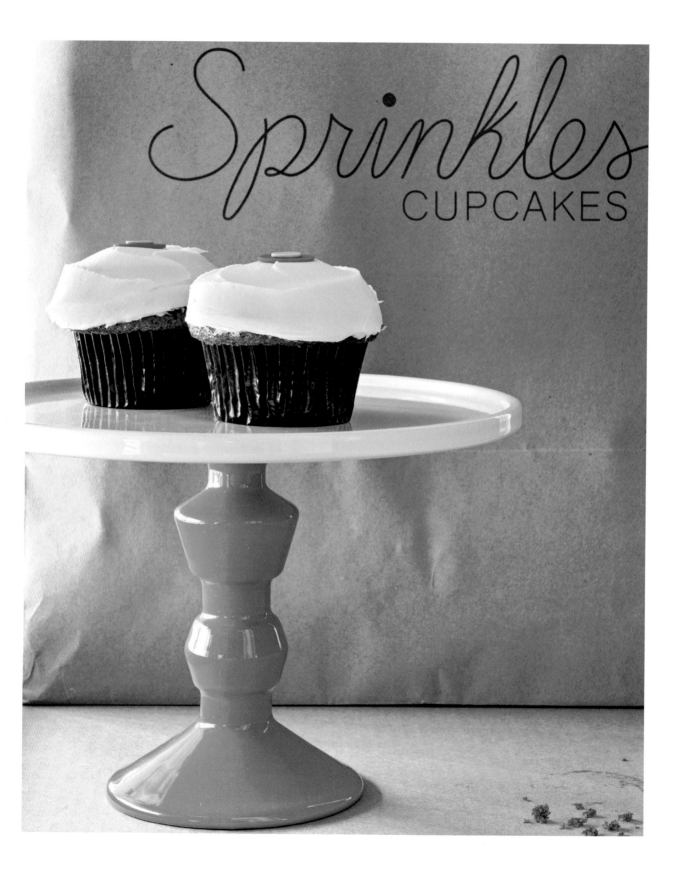

eggs one at a time, and beat until creamy, 1 to 2 minutes. Slowly add half the flour mixture, then the buttermilk mixture, then the remaining flour mixture, beating until just blended after each addition.

Divide the batter evenly among the liners and bake until the tops are just dry to the touch and a toothpick inserted into the center comes out clean, 17 to 19 minutes. Transfer the pan to a wire rack and let cool completely before frosting with cream cheese frosting.

BAKING TIME

If I were to boil down the key to a great-tasting cupcake, the secret—besides a stellar recipe, of course—would be baking time. At the store, we have it down to a science, tapping the top of the cupcake in the center of the pan the way a grillmaster might check the doneness of a fine steak. But we can do this because we've baked these recipes millions of times! To help give you that same confidence, I have tested all these recipes time and again, in every sort of oven, in kitchens across America, to try to nail that perfect baking time. Having said that, every oven is different, every city has a different climate and altitude, and ingredients and even stand mixers vary widely. (And if you have a convection oven, reduce the recipe temperature by 25 degrees for the same amount of time.) Although I am not a huge fan of the "toothpick test," I realize it has value when you're making something for the first time. So go ahead—use the baking time guidelines, the toothpick test, and your sense of smell to know when the cupcakes are done. Then, write notes in the margins of this book. Date it. Mark your baking times. Repeat your favorites. Soon enough, these recipes will feel like second nature, and you'll be baking cupcakes intuitively like a Sprinkles pro.

TO BAKE AS A CAKE

Butter two 9-inch round cake pans, line the bottoms with parchment paper cut to fit, and butter the parchment. Flour the pans, coating the bottom and sides of each pan, then tap out the excess flour. Divide the batter between the two pans and bake until the tops are dry to the touch, the sides of the cake start to pull away from the pan, and a toothpick inserted into the center comes out clean (for generally the same amount of time as in the cupcake recipe). Let cool on a wire rack, then remove each cake from its pan, discard the parchment paper, and set one cake layer on a cake round, frosting turntable, or the final serving platter. Frost the top of that cake layer with the frosting, stack the second layer on top, and frost the top and sides with the remaining frosting.

FOOD COLORING

Like me, you probably grew up using liquid food coloring from the little supermarket four-pack (red, yellow, blue, green). These days, I prefer to use **gel-based food coloring**, as it gives me more control over the tinting process. I prefer Flow Paste by Kopykake or Americolor soft gel paste food coloring, both of which can be purchased at cake decorating stores or on Amazon, but Wilton and Betty Crocker also make gel food colors you can often find at your local grocery store. Just make sure not to confuse gel food coloring with decorating (or writing) gel; the latter is a translucent gel meant for writing messages on the top of cakes and cookies.

A few pro tips I learned after much trial and error:

Gel-based coloring can cling to measuring implements. When mixing the liquid components for a cupcake that uses gel-based coloring, use the measuring spoon itself to stir the mixture; that way you'll ensure it all gets incorporated.

When working with food coloring, know that stains are a possibility; work as neatly and carefully as possible (and wear an apron with extra coverage) to make sure your hands, fingertips, clothes, and countertops don't acquire a semipermanent shade of red!

HOW TO FROST A CUPCAKE

At Sprinkles, we shun the pastry bag and hand-frost each and every cupcake using an offset spatula. This method is incredibly labor-intensive, but the result is rewarding, as it preserves the frosting's rich and creamy texture. A few important tips: Hold your cupcake lightly at its base with your fingertips. Beware of the "death grip"—squeezing a freshly baked cupcake may crush its tender crumb! Using your spatula, scoop a heaping dollop of frosting on top of the cupcake. Ideally, you want to start with more than you think you will need, since it's easier to scrape away some rather than adding more. Pat the frosting down and smooth it to the edges, using a back-and-forth motion with the back side of the spatula blade. Then spin the spatula's blade around the circumference of the cupcake top, moving the frosting toward you as you turn the cupcake away from you. Remove excess frosting from the blade by scraping it onto the edge of your frosting bowl and repeat. Just a few swirls should be enough. The less you work the frosting, the cleaner it looks! And most of all, don't get discouraged...our bakery employees frost thousands of cupcakes before perfecting our signature Sprinkles swirl!

ABOUT SPRINKLES FROSTING

My signature frosting recipes are made in the style of "American buttercream." Part of their beauty is in their simplicity: butter, confectioners' sugar, salt, and vanilla are the building blocks for a classic, user-friendly frosting that requires no cooking, but still makes for a super-smooth, silky frosting experience. There are a few things to remember when making my frostings:

Confectioners' sugar must be sifted. This extra step yields the smoothest texture.

Use fresh unsalted butter. This allows you to control the amount of salt that goes into the frosting recipe.

Butter should be slightly cooler than room temperature. It should feel cool, but give way to the press of a finger.

Use fine-grain sea salt. It dissolves well, which will give the frosting the smoothest texture.

Use best-quality vanilla extract. This can really make or break a recipe, especially one with so few ingredients. As always, I choose Nielsen-Massey (see Pantry, page 6).

Use a stand mixer if you can for maximum control and steady power. But if you don't have one, a handheld mixer will also work. The key is to break up the butter by beating it until just smooth before adding the other ingredients.

Keep the mixer on medium-low speed. Maintaining a low yet steady speed while mixing the ingredients prevents excess air from being incorporated into the frosting. By design, Sprinkles frostings are dense and luxuriously creamy like high-quality ice cream—not overly airy.

All the frosting recipes yield enough to frost 12 cupcakes or 1 2-layer 9-inch cake.

VANILLA MILK CHOCOLATE CUPCAKES

MAKES 12 CUPCAKES OR ONE 2-LAYER 9-INCH CAKE

A favorite with kids, this recipe takes our classic vanilla cupcake and pairs it with a fudgy milk chocolate frosting. While milk chocolate's qualities can sometimes feel diluted, I wanted to find a way to reflect it perfectly in a frosting. Upon remembering that top-quality chocolatiers make milk chocolate by adding milk solids to dark chocolate, I borrowed the method and mellowed a dark chocolate frosting base with cream cheese, yielding a mightier milk chocolate experience.

1½ cups all-purpose flour

1 teaspoon baking powder

¼ teaspoon baking soda

¼ teaspoon fine sea salt

⅔ cup whole milk

1½ teaspoons pure vanilla extract

½ cup (1 stick) unsalted butter, slightly softened

1 cup sugar

1 large egg

2 large egg whites

Milk Chocolate Cream Cheese Frosting

Preheat the oven to 325°F. Line a 12-cup cupcake pan with paper liners.

In a medium bowl, whisk together the flour, baking powder, baking soda, and salt. In a small bowl, stir together the milk and vanilla.

In the bowl of a stand mixer fitted with the paddle attachment, beat the butter and sugar on medium-high speed until light and fluffy, 2 to 3 minutes. Reduce the speed to medium-low, slowly add the egg and egg whites one at a time, and beat until creamy, 1 to 2 minutes. Slowly add half the flour mixture, then the milk mixture, then the remaining flour mixture, beating until just blended after each addition.

Divide the batter evenly among the liners and bake until the tops are just dry to the touch and a toothpick inserted into the center comes out clean, 18 to 20 minutes. Transfer the pan to a wire rack and cool completely before frosting with milk chocolate cream cheese frosting.

✳ To bake as a cake, see the box on page 16.

MILK CHOCOLATE CREAM CHEESE FROSTING

MAKES 1¾ CUPS

1 (8-ounce) package cream cheese, slightly softened

½ cup (1 stick) unsalted butter, slightly softened

⅛ teaspoon fine sea salt

3 ounces bittersweet chocolate, melted, still slightly warm

2 cups confectioners' sugar, sifted

1 tablespoon whole milk, plus more as needed

½ teaspoon pure vanilla extract

In the bowl of a stand mixer fitted with the paddle attachment, beat the cream cheese, butter, and salt on medium-high speed until light and fluffy, 2 to 3 minutes. Slowly add the melted chocolate and beat for 1 minute more. Reduce the speed to low and gradually add the confectioners' sugar until just incorporated, being careful not to beat too much air into the frosting. Add the milk and vanilla and beat until just blended. If necessary, add more milk 1 tablespoon at a time until the frosting has a spreadable consistency but is still thick and fudgy.

COCONUT CUPCAKES

MAKES 12 CUPCAKES OR ONE 2-LAYER 9-INCH CAKE

There is something ethereal about a coconut cupcake in its flurry of white: snowy coconut cake, fluffy coconut cream cheese frosting, and a drift of sweetened coconut shreds. Elegant and pared down, yet utterly simple and childlike in the messy imperfection of those coconut shreds, it's both true sophistication and sweet innocence in one little package. I use coconut milk in the cake to add richness, then bump up the subtle coconut flavor with a small amount of coconut extract—look for as pure a product as you can find.

1½ cups all-purpose flour

1 teaspoon baking powder

¼ teaspoon baking soda

¼ teaspoon fine sea salt

⅔ cup full-fat canned coconut milk, whisked to emulsify the solids and liquids

1 teaspoon pure vanilla extract

½ teaspoon coconut extract

½ cup (1 stick) unsalted butter, slightly softened

1 cup sugar

2 large eggs

Coconut Cream Cheese Frosting

¾ cup sweetened shredded coconut shavings, for garnish

Preheat the oven to 325°F. Line a 12-cup cupcake pan with paper liners.

In a medium bowl, whisk together the flour, baking powder, baking soda, and salt. In a small bowl, stir together the coconut milk with the vanilla and coconut extracts.

In the bowl of a stand mixer fitted with the paddle attachment, beat the butter and sugar on medium-high speed until light and fluffy, 2 to 3 minutes. Reduce the speed to medium-low, add the eggs one at a time, and beat until creamy, 1 to 2 minutes. Slowly add half the flour mixture, then the coconut milk mixture, then the remaining flour mixture, beating until just blended after each addition.

Divide the batter evenly among the liners and bake until the tops are just dry to the touch and a toothpick inserted into the center comes out clean, 17 to 19 minutes. Transfer the pan to a wire rack and cool completely before frosting with coconut cream cheese frosting.

✳ To bake as a cake, see the box on page 16.

COCONUT CREAM CHEESE FROSTING

MAKES 2 CUPS

1 (8-ounce) package cream cheese, slightly softened

½ cup (1 stick) unsalted butter, slightly softened

⅛ teaspoon fine sea salt

3¾ cups confectioners' sugar, sifted

¾ teaspoon coconut extract

¼ teaspoon pure vanilla extract

In the bowl of a stand mixer fitted with the paddle attachment, beat the cream cheese, butter, and salt on medium speed until light and fluffy, 2 minutes. Reduce the speed to low, gradually add the confectioners' sugar, and beat until incorporated. Increase the speed to medium, add the coconut and vanilla extracts, and beat until fully blended, 1 to 2 minutes, making sure not to incorporate too much air into the frosting.

BLACK AND WHITE CUPCAKES

MAKES 12 CUPCAKES OR 1 2-LAYER 9-INCH CAKE

A best seller at our stores, this marriage of bittersweet dark chocolate cake and vanilla frosting creates a yin-yang of flavors that's so, so good—and my husband Charles's hands-down favorite. Like the iced black and white cookies you find all over New York City or a frosty milk shake that mixes vanilla and chocolate ice creams, this flavor combination is a classic for a reason. If you need to choose one cupcake to serve at a party, go with this one—it's a crowd-pleaser!

1 cup all-purpose flour

⅔ cup unsweetened cocoa powder

¾ teaspoon baking powder

½ teaspoon baking soda

½ teaspoon fine sea salt

⅔ cup buttermilk, shaken

1 teaspoon pure vanilla extract

10 tablespoons (1¼ sticks) unsalted butter, slightly softened

⅔ cup sugar

⅓ cup lightly packed light brown sugar

2 large eggs

Vanilla Frosting

Preheat the oven to 350°F. Line a 12-cup cupcake pan with paper liners.

In a medium bowl, whisk together the flour, cocoa powder, baking powder, baking soda, and salt. In a small bowl, stir together the buttermilk and vanilla.

In the bowl of a stand mixer fitted with the paddle attachment, beat the butter and both sugars on medium-high speed until light and fluffy, 2 to 3 minutes. Reduce the speed to medium-low, add the eggs one at a time, and beat until creamy, 1 to 2 minutes. Slowly add half the flour mixture, then the buttermilk mixture, then the remaining flour mixture, beating until just blended after each addition.

Divide the batter evenly among the liners and bake until the tops are just dry to the touch and a toothpick inserted into the center comes out clean, 18 to 20 minutes. Transfer the pan to a wire rack and cool completely before frosting with vanilla frosting.

＊ To bake as a cake, see the box on page 16.

VANILLA FROSTING

MAKES 2 CUPS

1 cup (2 sticks) unsalted butter, slightly softened

⅛ teaspoon fine sea salt

3 cups confectioners' sugar, sifted

5 teaspoons whole milk

1 teaspoon pure vanilla extract

In the bowl of a stand mixer fitted with the paddle attachment, beat the butter and salt on medium speed until light and fluffy, 2 minutes. Reduce the speed to low, gradually add the confectioners' sugar, and beat until incorporated. Increase the speed to medium, add the milk and vanilla, and beat until fully blended, 1 to 2 minutes, making sure not to incorporate too much air into the frosting.

CARROT CUPCAKES

MAKES 12 CUPCAKES OR ONE 2-LAYER 9-INCH CAKE

This cupcake is loaded with gobs of freshly grated carrots to take advantage of their natural, visual appeal and many cake-enhancing qualities. Carrots' naturally high sugar and water content encourage a sweet and extra-lush cake . . . and their bright-orange hue offers cheery bursts of color in every bite. Buttermilk helps make this cupcake extra moist, but still light and fluffy and without any of the leaden gumminess you sometimes get with carrot cupcakes. And though some can't imagine a carrot cake without raisins, I prefer just the crunch of toasted walnuts. The crowning glory is a sweet and tangy cinnamon cream cheese frosting, which adds extra spice and perfect balance.

1½ cups all-purpose flour	¾ cup vegetable oil
2 teaspoons ground cinnamon	¼ cup buttermilk, shaken
½ teaspoon freshly grated nutmeg	2 large eggs
1 teaspoon baking powder	1 teaspoon pure vanilla extract
¼ teaspoon baking soda	2 large carrots, finely grated (1¾ cups grated)
½ teaspoon fine sea salt	⅓ cup chopped toasted walnuts
1 cup lightly packed light brown sugar	Cinnamon Cream Cheese Frosting

Preheat the oven to 350°F. Line a 12-cup cupcake pan with paper liners.

In a medium bowl, whisk together the flour, cinnamon, nutmeg, baking powder, baking soda, and salt.

In the bowl of a stand mixer fitted with the paddle attachment, beat the brown sugar, oil, buttermilk, eggs, and vanilla on medium-high speed until smooth, 1 minute. Reduce the speed to low and add half the flour mixture, then the carrots and the walnuts, then the remaining flour mixture, beating until just blended after each addition.

Divide the batter evenly among the liners and bake until the tops are just dry to the touch and a toothpick inserted into the center comes out clean, 21 to 23 minutes. Transfer the pan to a wire rack and cool completely before frosting with cinnamon cream cheese frosting.

Garnish with carrot curls, if desired.

✳ To bake as a cake, see the box on page 16.

CINNAMON CREAM CHEESE FROSTING

MAKES 2 CUPS

1 (8-ounce) package cream cheese, slightly softened

½ cup (1 stick) unsalted butter, slightly softened

⅛ teaspoon fine sea salt

3¾ cups confectioners' sugar, sifted

1½ teaspoons ground cinnamon

¼ teaspoon pure vanilla extract

In the bowl of a stand mixer fitted with the paddle attachment, beat the cream cheese, butter, and salt on medium speed until light and fluffy, 2 minutes. Reduce the speed to low, gradually add the confectioners' sugar, and beat until incorporated. Increase the speed to medium, add the cinnamon and vanilla, and beat until fully blended, 1 to 2 minutes, making sure not to incorporate too much air into the frosting.

PEANUT BUTTER CHIP CUPCAKES

MAKES 12 CUPCAKES OR ONE 2-LAYER 9-INCH CAKE

A hearty, seriously dense cupcake studded with dark chocolate chips, my peanut butter creation is not for the faint of heart. It's been an especially popular choice among our male customer base ever since its creation and, for me, always brings back distinct childhood memories of my dad eating peanut butter by the spoonful. We use an all-natural peanut butter in both the cake and the frosting, making this a potently peanutty experience; just be sure to stir the oil that often rises to the top of the jar fully back into the peanut butter before using; the fat is essential to the consistency of both the cupcake and the frosting. And don't worry if the cupcake liners seem extra full before baking; this rich batter doesn't rise as much as other batters in this book.

1½ cups all-purpose flour

1½ teaspoons baking powder

¼ teaspoon fine sea salt

¾ cup buttermilk, shaken

1½ teaspoons pure vanilla extract

½ cup (1 stick) unsalted butter, slightly softened

¾ cup lightly packed dark brown sugar

⅔ cup unsalted natural creamy peanut butter, such as Laura Scudder's, well stirred

2 large eggs

¾ cup semisweet chocolate chips

Peanut Butter Frosting

Preheat the oven to 350°F. Line a 12-cup cupcake pan with paper liners.

In a medium bowl, whisk together the flour, baking powder, and salt. In a small bowl, stir together the buttermilk and vanilla.

In the bowl of a stand mixer fitted with the paddle attachment, beat the butter, brown sugar, and peanut butter on medium-high speed until light and fluffy, 2 to 3 minutes. Reduce the speed to medium-low, add the eggs one at a time, and beat until creamy, 1 to 2 minutes. Slowly add half the flour mixture, then the buttermilk mixture, then the remaining flour mixture, beating until just blended after each addition. Stir in the chocolate chips.

Divide the batter evenly among the liners (the batter will come to the very tops of the liners) and bake until the tops are just dry to the touch and a toothpick inserted into the center comes out clean, 18 to 20 minutes. Transfer the pan to a wire rack and cool completely before frosting with peanut butter frosting.

✳ To bake as a cake, see the box on page 16.

PEANUT BUTTER FROSTING

MAKES 2 CUPS

¾ cup (1½ sticks) unsalted butter, room temperature

¾ cup unsalted natural, creamy peanut butter, such as Laura Scudder's, well stirred

¼ teaspoon fine sea salt

1½ cups confectioners' sugar, sifted

1 tablespoon whole milk

In the bowl of a stand mixer fitted with the paddle attachment, beat the butter, peanut butter, and salt on medium-high speed until creamy, 1 to 2 minutes. Reduce the speed to low, gradually add the confectioners' sugar, and beat until just incorporated. Add the milk, increase the speed to medium-high, and beat until the frosting is light and spreadable, 1 to 2 minutes.

DARK CHOCOLATE CUPCAKES

MAKES 12 CUPCAKES OR ONE 2-LAYER 9-INCH CAKE

Charles's mom, Lynda, and I share a passion for this particular Sprinkles cupcake. Any time we are together, our Sprinkles boxes are heavy on the dark chocolate—neither one of us wants to be the one to disappoint the other by taking the last one! Although I have had infatuations with each Sprinkles flavor for periods of time, Lynda is a loyalist and has never once strayed. Her standing order is known by our cupcake associates from Beverly Hills to Scottsdale to New York. This cupcake's deep chocolate flavor is thanks to a heavy dose of cocoa; the velvety texture comes from the buttermilk, as well as an always-light hand when mixing the batter and baking the final product. Chocolate on chocolate is always a classic and some things, like Lynda's order, never change!

1 cup all-purpose flour

⅔ cup unsweetened cocoa powder

¾ teaspoon baking powder

½ teaspoon baking soda

½ teaspoon fine sea salt

⅔ cup buttermilk, shaken

1 teaspoon pure vanilla extract

10 tablespoons (1¼ sticks) unsalted butter, slightly softened

⅔ cup sugar

⅓ cup lightly packed light brown sugar

2 large eggs

Dark Chocolate Frosting

Preheat the oven to 350°F. Line a 12-cup cupcake pan with paper liners.

In a medium bowl, whisk together the flour, cocoa powder, baking powder, baking soda, and salt. In a small bowl, stir together the buttermilk and vanilla.

In the bowl of a stand mixer fitted with the paddle attachment, beat the butter and both sugars on medium-high speed until light and fluffy, 2 to 3 minutes. Reduce the speed to medium-low, add the eggs one at a time, and beat until creamy, 1 to 2 minutes. Slowly add half the flour mixture, then the buttermilk mixture, then the remaining flour mixture, beating until just blended after each addition.

Divide the batter evenly among the liners and bake until the tops are just dry to the touch and a toothpick inserted into the center comes out clean, 18 to 20 minutes. Transfer the pan to a wire rack and cool completely before frosting with dark chocolate frosting.

✳ To bake as a cake, see the box on page 16.

DARK CHOCOLATE FROSTING

MAKES 2 CUPS

¾ cup (1½ sticks) unsalted butter, slightly softened

⅛ teaspoon fine sea salt

2½ cups confectioners' sugar, sifted

¼ teaspoon pure vanilla extract

6 ounces bittersweet chocolate, melted and cooled to room temperature

2 tablespoons whole milk, if necessary

In the bowl of a stand mixer fitted with the paddle attachment, beat the butter and salt on medium speed until fluffy, 1 to 2 minutes. Gradually add the confectioners' sugar and beat until smooth, 2 to 3 minutes. Add the vanilla and melted chocolate and beat until just incorporated, being careful not to incorporate too much air into the frosting. Add milk 1 tablespoon at a time, if needed, to achieve a spreadable consistency.

WORKING WITH FONDANT

Sprinkles Cupcakes are known worldwide for their signature modern dot decorations, a contemporary play on a traditional "sprinkle." Our modern dot is made of one smaller dot inside a larger dot in two different hues.

It's simple to make your own signature edible shapes for your cupcakes at home with fondant, the pliable and eminently versatile decorating material I like to think of as the pastry world's edible Play-Doh. Though colored fondants are available, I recommend purchasing white fondant and coloring it with food coloring gels so you can play with various shades. Start with a ball of fondant about half the size of your fist, then add a couple drops of coloring gel to the center and begin kneading

it in. Kneading helps distribute the color, but also warms the fondant into a workable consistency. You will see the fondant take on color quickly; add more color, a drop or two at a time. Once you achieve your desired hue, use a fondant rolling pin (typically small and plastic) to roll it out to about ⅛ inch thick. It is helpful to roll on a Silpat (a nonstick silicone mat) or to sprinkle a dash of confectioners' sugar on the fondant to avoid sticking. Now for the best part! Use tiny fondant cutters or cookie cutters to create fun shapes. Don't limit yourself to 2-D shapes; fondant can be hand molded into virtually any shape. One of my favorites: creating roses by rolling thin, folded strips of pink fondant into tiny buds!

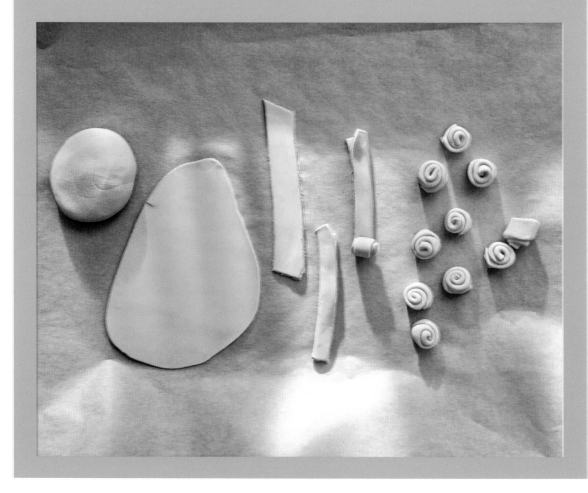

HOW TO EAT A CUPCAKE

Everyone has their own way of eating a Sprinkles cupcake; over the past eleven years, I've truly seen it all. Here are a few methods learned either by experience or observation.

The Lollipop: Savor every moment by licking the frosting off the top like a kid eating a lollipop.

The 10-Second Oven: Pop your cupcake in the microwave and zap for a few seconds to create a melty, fresh-from-the-oven effect.

The Frosting Sandwich: Twist off the cupcake bottom from the top, flip the top over, and place it on the cupcake bottom so that the frosting is sandwiched between layers of cake.

The Pro: Remove the cupcake wrapper and hold the cupcake level with your mouth, ensuring that you consume proportional amounts of cake and frosting with each bite.

Miss Manners: Eating a cupcake with a fork and knife is completely acceptable. It also helps you gather every last crumb; press the fork's tines onto the crumbs to swoop them up!

Halvesies: Cut your cupcake straight down the middle. Have your friend do the same. Exchange one half and re-form your cupcake to enjoy the best of both worlds. Best enjoyed with a close buddy—or someone you want to get to know better.

VANILLA CUPCAKES

MAKES 12 CUPCAKES OR ONE 2-LAYER 9-INCH CAKE

For purists, nothing equals our vanilla cupcake. It was the first recipe I created for Sprinkles, and it has been a crowd favorite from the start. I reduced the number of egg yolks here to allow the vanilla's creamy, floral characteristics to shine through. I've been using Nielsen-Massey Madagascar Bourbon vanilla—in my opinion, the world's finest—since day one, because nothing else matches its unadulterated flavor profile. If you can find it, I highly recommend it. But no matter what brand you choose, make sure it's pure vanilla extract.

* To bake as a cake, see the box on page 16.

1½ cups all-purpose flour

1 teaspoon baking powder

¼ teaspoon baking soda

¼ teaspoon fine sea salt

⅔ cup whole milk

1½ teaspoons pure vanilla extract

½ cup (1 stick) unsalted butter, slightly softened

1 cup sugar

1 large egg

2 large egg whites

Vanilla Frosting (page 25)

Preheat the oven to 325°F. Line a 12-cup cupcake pan with paper liners.

In a medium bowl, whisk together the flour, baking powder, baking soda, and salt. In a small bowl, stir together the milk and vanilla.

In the bowl of a stand mixer fitted with the paddle attachment, beat the butter and sugar on medium-high speed until light and fluffy, 2 to 3 minutes. Reduce the speed to medium-low, slowly add the egg and egg whites one at a time, and beat until creamy, 1 to 2 minutes. Slowly add half the flour mixture, then the milk mixture, then the remaining flour mixture, beating until just blended after each addition.

Divide the batter evenly among the cupcake liners and bake until the tops are just dry to the touch, and a toothpick inserted into the center comes out clean, 18 to 20 minutes. Transfer the pan to a wire rack and cool completely before frosting with vanilla frosting.

STRAWBERRY CUPCAKES

MAKES 12 CUPCAKES OR ONE 2-LAYER 9-INCH CAKE

My husband grew up in Oklahoma City, where strawberry cake is as much a staple as desserts that celebrate chocolate and vanilla. It was a new one to me, but over the years it has become a personal favorite. The one from Alberta's Tea Room (now closed), where all the Oklahoma City ladies went to socialize and dine on chicken tetrazzini, was famous, and that's the version I used as inspiration for this cupcake, which has become a customer favorite at Sprinkles. The subtle flavor of the pureed strawberries in the cupcake batter adds a fresh, summery flavor, reinforced by more strawberry in the frosting. I should add that this is the cupcake I made with Martha Stewart on her show; after years of watching her bake perfect desserts on TV, it was a pinch-me moment and a highlight of my career.

1½ cups all-purpose flour, sifted

1 teaspoon baking powder

¼ teaspoon fine sea salt

¾ cup whole hulled fresh or frozen strawberries (thawed if frozen)

¼ cup whole milk, at room temperature

1 teaspoon pure vanilla extract

½ cup (1 stick) unsalted butter, slightly softened

1 cup sugar

1 large egg, at room temperature

2 large egg whites, at room temperature

Strawberry Frosting

Preheat the oven to 350°F. Line a 12-cup cupcake pan with paper liners.

In a medium bowl, whisk together the flour, baking powder, and salt.

In a food processor (or mini chopper), puree the strawberries until smooth. Transfer to a small bowl and stir in the milk and vanilla.

In the bowl of a stand mixer fitted with the paddle attachment, beat the butter and sugar on medium-high speed until light and fluffy, 2 to 3 minutes. Reduce the speed to medium-low, add the egg and egg whites one at a time, and beat until creamy, 1 to 2 minutes. Slowly add half the flour mixture, then the milk mixture, then the remaining flour mixture, beating until just blended after each addition. Divide the batter evenly among the liners and bake until the tops are just dry to the touch and a toothpick inserted into the center comes out clean, 21 to 23 minutes. Transfer the pan to a wire rack and cool completely before frosting with strawberry frosting.

* To bake as a cake, see the box on page 16.

STRAWBERRY FROSTING

MAKES 2 CUPS

¼ cup whole hulled fresh or frozen strawberries (thawed if frozen)

1 cup (2 sticks) unsalted butter, slightly softened

⅛ teaspoon fine sea salt

3½ cups confectioners' sugar, sifted

½ teaspoon pure vanilla extract

In a small food processor (or mini chopper), puree the strawberries until smooth. Measure out 3 tablespoons of the puree.

In the bowl of a stand mixer fitted with the paddle attachment, beat the butter and salt on medium speed until light and fluffy, 1 to 2 minutes. Reduce the speed to low, gradually add the confectioners' sugar, and beat until creamy, 1 to 2 minutes. Add the vanilla and the 3 tablespoons strawberry puree and beat until blended, making sure not to incorporate too much air into the frosting.

THE CUPCAKE ATM ENGAGEMENT

One of my favorite #sprinklesmoments was the product of careful planning and a cupcake-filled courtship. Our customer Ray emailed Sprinkles asking if we could help him propose to his girlfriend, Adria. Sprinkles had played a starring role in their love story, and Ray wanted to include us in his proposal. We got our entire Beverly Hills store on board and laid out a plan down to the minute. We traded out Adria's favorite cupcake—S'more—for a ring Ray discreetly slipped us minutes in advance. As Ray and Adria walked up to the Cupcake ATM, we were in the kitchen monitoring everything on our security cameras. As planned, Adria ordered a box expecting a S'more cupcake, but received a sparkling engagement ring instead. Ray turned to Adria, got down on one knee, and popped the question. "Yes!" she said. "But where's my cupcake?"

GLUTEN FREE RED VELVET CUPCAKES

MAKES 12 CUPCAKES OR ONE 2-LAYER 9-INCH CAKE

Gluten-free baking is here to stay; just ask the legions of customers who practically begged us to create a gluten-free version of our most iconic flavor. When I set out to develop this recipe, it was essential that it not only pass muster, but rank up there with the taste experience of the original, signature red velvet cupcake. Traditional wheat-flour cupcakes contain gluten, which is an integral element in developing the structure of many baked goods. The trick was to find that perfect substitute in the form of a great, gluten-free blend. At Sprinkles, we make our own custom blend, but there are plenty of great packaged gluten-free flour blends to choose from. I tested as many varieties as I could find, eventually landing on Cup4Cup gluten-free flour. It creates a delicate crumb without any of the unpleasant flavors that can accompany gluten-free flours. These cupcakes can bake up a little funky, without the symmetrical domed top of most of our other recipes. Luckily, any visual imperfections are hidden by a thick layer of frosting; and, thank goodness, our classic cream cheese frosting recipe is naturally gluten-free!

1½ cups gluten-free flour blend, preferably Cup4Cup brand

3 tablespoons unsweetened cocoa powder

¾ teaspoon baking soda

¾ teaspoon fine sea salt

¼ cup buttermilk, shaken

¼ cup room-temperature water

1½ teaspoons distilled white vinegar

1 teaspoon pure vanilla extract

¾ teaspoon red gel food coloring (see page 17)

10 tablespoons (1¼ sticks) unsalted butter, slightly softened

¾ cup sugar

¼ cup lightly packed light brown sugar

2 large eggs

Cream Cheese Frosting (page 14)

Preheat the oven to 350°F. Line a 12-cup cupcake pan with paper liners.

In a medium bowl, whisk together the flour, cocoa powder, baking soda, and salt. In a small bowl, stir together the buttermilk, water, vinegar, vanilla, and food coloring.

In the bowl of a stand mixer fitted with the paddle attachment, beat the butter and both sugars on medium-high speed until light and fluffy, 2 to 3 minutes. Reduce the speed to medium-low, add the eggs one at a time, and beat until creamy, 1 to 2 minutes. Slowly add half the flour mixture, then the buttermilk mixture, then the remaining flour mixture, beating until just blended after each addition.

Divide the batter evenly among the liners and bake until the tops are just dry to the touch and a toothpick inserted into the center comes out clean, 17 to 19 minutes. Transfer the pan to a wire rack and cool completely before frosting with cream cheese frosting.

* To bake as a cake, see the box on page 16.

VEGAN RED VELVET CUPCAKES

MAKES 12 CUPCAKES OR ONE 2-LAYER 9-INCH CAKE

When people ask how I come up with Sprinkles recipes, I always tell them I just create what I personally love to eat! But early in the company's life, it became clear that there were people with dietary concerns who couldn't indulge in our cupcakes even if they really, *really* wanted to. So I set about re-creating our most popular flavor in an animal product–free format. Vegans rejoiced, and word spread far and wide. Today, this awesome red velvet is beloved by some of the most famous vegans in LA—and sometimes preferred over the original recipe by non-vegans! Word to the wise: When creating these, make sure all of the liquid components are at room temperature; this prevents the coconut oil from seizing up. The frosting will be slightly looser than a typical Sprinkles frosting, but tastes just as good. As in all of our recipes, make sure the cupcakes are completely cool before frosting.

1½ cups all-purpose flour

3 tablespoons unsweetened cocoa powder

¾ teaspoon baking soda

¾ teaspoon fine sea salt

⅔ cup sweetened plain soy milk

1½ teaspoons distilled white vinegar

1 teaspoon pure vanilla extract

¾ teaspoon red gel food coloring (see page 17)

⅔ cup coconut oil (plus more for greasing if making into a cake)

1¼ cups coconut palm sugar*

½ cup unsweetened applesauce

Vegan Cream Cheese Frosting

Preheat the oven to 350°F. Line a 12-cup cupcake pan with paper liners.

In a medium bowl, whisk together the flour, cocoa powder, baking soda, and salt. In a small bowl, stir together the soy milk, vinegar, vanilla, and food coloring.

In the bowl of a stand mixer fitted with the paddle attachment, beat the coconut oil and coconut palm sugar on medium-high speed until light and fluffy, 2 to 3 minutes. Reduce the speed to medium-low, add the applesauce, and beat until creamy, 1 to 2 minutes. Slowly add half the flour mixture, then the soy milk mixture, then the remaining flour mixture, beating until just blended after each addition.

✱ Available at health food stores.

VEGAN CREAM CHEESE FROSTING

MAKES 2 CUPS

1 (8-ounce) package vegan cream cheese, such as Tofutti, slightly cold

3¾ cups (a 1-pound box) confectioners' sugar, sifted

¼ cup coconut oil, melted to liquid form, but not warm

½ teaspoon pure vanilla extract

¼ teaspoon fine sea salt

In the bowl of a stand mixer fitted with the paddle attachment, beat the vegan cream cheese on medium speed until light and fluffy, 1 to 2 minutes. Reduce the speed to low and gradually add the confectioners' sugar, 1 cup at a time, until incorporated. Slowly add the liquid coconut oil until creamy. Add the vanilla and salt, increase the speed to medium, and beat until fully blended, 1 to 2 minutes, being careful not to incorporate too much air into the frosting.

Divide the batter evenly among the liners and bake until the tops are just dry to the touch and a toothpick inserted into the center comes out clean, 16 to 18 minutes. Transfer the pan to a wire rack and cool completely before frosting with vegan cream cheese frosting.

✳ To bake as a cake, see the box on page 16. While this frosting is just as delicious as its non-vegan cousin, it holds its shape differently. So I recommend going "naked" here: simply frost the interior of the cake, and then the top—but leave the sides unfrosted.

CINNAMON SUGAR CUPCAKES

MAKES 12 CUPCAKES

The inspiration for these yummy cupcakes is the donut muffin from the Downtown Bakery & Creamery in Healdsburg, California, which I first discovered at the Ferry Plaza Farmers Market in San Francisco and loved so much that I dedicated an entire segment to them on Food Network's *The Best Thing I Ever Ate*. When I lived in San Francisco, I'd make a beeline for their stand, always slightly panicked that they might be sold out. So what better way to ensure a steady supply than to create my own version that I could bake up whenever I wanted? When transformed into a cupcake, the crumb becomes even more tender—but the cinnamon-sugar goodness remains exactly the same.

2 cups all-purpose flour

1¼ teaspoons baking powder

1 teaspoon ground cinnamon

½ teaspoon freshly grated nutmeg

¼ teaspoon baking soda

½ teaspoon fine sea salt

⅔ cup buttermilk, shaken

1 teaspoon pure vanilla extract

½ cup (1 stick) unsalted butter, slightly softened

⅓ cup sugar

1½ tablespoons lightly packed light brown sugar

2 large eggs

Preheat the oven to 350°F. Line a 12-cup cupcake pan with paper liners.

In a medium bowl, whisk together the flour, baking powder, cinnamon, nutmeg, baking soda, and salt. In a small bowl, stir together the buttermilk and vanilla.

In the bowl of a stand mixer fitted with the paddle attachment, beat the butter and both sugars on medium-high speed until light and fluffy, 2 to 3 minutes. Reduce the speed to medium-low, add the eggs one at a time, and beat until creamy, 1 to 2 minutes. Slowly add half the flour mixture, then the buttermilk mixture, then the remaining flour mixture, beating until just blended after each addition.

Divide the batter evenly among the liners and bake until the tops are just dry to the touch and a toothpick inserted into the center comes out clean, 21 to 23 minutes. Transfer the pan to a wire rack and cool completely.

CINNAMON SUGAR TOPPING

¼ cup sugar

1½ teaspoons ground cinnamon

4 tablespoons (½ stick) unsalted butter, melted

In a shallow bowl, combine the sugar and cinnamon. Brush the tops of the cupcakes with the melted butter, turn them upside down, and roll them in the cinnamon-sugar mixture, tilting them from side to side to cover as much of the top as possible. Invert and serve.

CHAPTER 3

FANCY CUPCAKES

In most cases, these cupcakes are slightly more ambitious than their "everyday" cousins, making them perfect for a special occasion that calls for a bit more wow factor. Others, like the Barbra Streisand cupcake, are not necessarily more labor-intensive, but there's something about the flavor combination or presentation that makes them elegant enough for a "fancy" affair. Don't be intimidated by the cupcakes with several elements, as components like curd, ganache, and frosting can all be made in advance. Just not the cupcake itself—a Sprinkles cupcake is always freshly baked!

CHOCOLATE MARSHMALLOW CUPCAKES

MAKES 12 CUPCAKES

Sprinkles hearts Stacey Winkler, one of Los Angeles' preeminent hostesses. Not only are Stacey's parties, with their lavish dessert tables, legendary events, but they're where my cupcakes made their debut when Sprinkles was still operating out of my West Hollywood duplex. Stacey and her husband, Henry Winkler (yes, *the* Henry Winkler), have been loyal customers from day one…and are now dear friends. The chocolate marshmallow cupcake is their favorite, and I have to say, they have great taste!! It's the grown-up version of the Hostess Ding Dong we all had in our lunch boxes, intended for people who like things a little less on the sweet side. A moist, chocolaty cupcake is paired with homemade marshmallow cream that will have you swearing off the jarred stuff for good. The ganache is simple to make—just make sure to use really good chocolate, since it's the crowning glory here.

FOR THE CUPCAKES:

1 cup all-purpose flour

⅔ cup unsweetened cocoa powder

¾ teaspoon baking powder

½ teaspoon baking soda

½ teaspoon fine sea salt

⅔ cup buttermilk, shaken

1 teaspoon pure vanilla extract

10 tablespoons (1¼ sticks) unsalted butter, slightly softened

⅔ cup sugar

⅓ cup lightly packed light brown sugar

2 large eggs

FOR THE MARSHMALLOW FROSTING:

1 cup sugar

¼ teaspoon cream of tartar

Pinch of fine sea salt

2 large egg whites

1 teaspoon pure vanilla extract

FOR THE CHOCOLATE GANACHE:

8 ounces semisweet chocolate, chopped into small pieces

1 cup heavy cream

(Continued)

MAKE THE CUPCAKES:

Preheat the oven to 350°F. Line a 12-cup cupcake pan with paper liners.

In a medium bowl, whisk together the flour, cocoa powder, baking powder, baking soda, and salt. In a small bowl, stir together the buttermilk and vanilla.

In the bowl of a stand mixer fitted with the paddle attachment, beat the butter and both sugars on medium-high speed until light and fluffy, 2 to 3 minutes. Reduce the speed to medium-low, add the eggs one at a time, and beat until creamy, 1 to 2 minutes. Slowly add half the flour mixture, then the buttermilk mixture, then the remaining flour mixture, beating until just blended after each addition.

Divide the batter evenly among the liners and bake until the tops are just dry to the touch and a toothpick inserted into the center comes out clean, 18 to 20 minutes. Transfer the pan to a wire rack and cool completely.

MAKE THE MARSHMALLOW FROSTING:

In a small, light-colored, stainless-steel saucepan, gently stir together ⅓ cup water, the sugar, cream of tartar, and salt. Begin to heat the mixture over medium heat without stirring.

Meanwhile, in the bowl of a stand mixer fitted with the whisk attachment, whip the egg whites on medium-high speed until soft peaks form, 2 minutes. Turn off the mixer but leave the whipped egg whites in the bowl.

Once the sugar mixture shows the first signs of bubbles and begins to boil, boil for exactly 3 minutes; the mixture will become thicker, the sugar will dissolve, and small bubbles will form on the surface of the sugar. Do not stir! (If the mixture begins to turn a faint yellow color, you have boiled too long.)

With the mixer on medium speed, slowly stream the hot sugar syrup into the egg whites, being careful to avoid the whisk (the syrup can harden into candy strands). Increase the speed to high and beat until stiff peaks form, about 7 minutes. During the last 15 seconds, beat in the vanilla until just incorporated. (If not using right away, store in a cool part of your kitchen counter in a glass or plastic container, with plastic wrap pressed directly over the frosting, and sealed with a tight lid.)

MAKE THE GANACHE:

Place the chocolate in a medium bowl. In a medium saucepan, bring the cream just to a boil. Pour the cream over the chocolate and let sit for 1 minute, then gently stir (don't stir vigorously; this adds too much air to the ganache) until the chocolate has melted and the ganache is smooth.

FILL AND FROST THE CUPCAKES:

Using a small, sharp knife, cut a circular hole into the center of each cupcake to create a hole about 1½ inches wide (reserve the scoops for snacking!), making sure not to dig too deep into the cupcake so the filling does not leak out the bottom. Fill each cupcake with 1½ tablespoons of the marshmallow frosting. Dunk the top of each cupcake into the ganache and quickly turn right-side up, cleaning any drips from the side. Allow the cupcakes to set at room temperature for 30 to 45 minutes. If desired, dunk the tops in ganache a second time for extra coverage and let set until dry.

CHAI LATTE CUPCAKES

MAKES 12 CUPCAKES OR ONE 2-LAYER 9-INCH CAKE

I am a huge fan of humorist Joel Stein's writing, so imagine my delight when he interviewed me for a *Time* magazine piece on the subject of—you guessed it—cupcakes. During our chat, he mentioned that the chai cupcake was his favorite Sprinkles flavor...just as we were considering taking it off the menu since it had a much smaller (though still very passionate) following then. But Joel single-handedly changed chai's fate, and I'm so glad he did, because this cupcake is delicious. Its perfect combination of spices creates the baked equivalent of a steaming chai latte.

1½ cups all-purpose flour

½ teaspoon ground cinnamon

½ teaspoon ground allspice

½ teaspoon ground ginger

¼ teaspoon ground cloves

¼ teaspoon ground cardamom

Pinch of freshly ground black pepper

1 teaspoon baking powder

¼ teaspoon fine sea salt

⅔ cup whole milk

½ teaspoon pure vanilla extract

½ cup (1 stick) unsalted butter, slightly softened

1 cup sugar

2 large eggs

Chai Latte Frosting

Preheat the oven to 325°F. Line a 12-cup cupcake pan with paper liners.

In a medium bowl, whisk together the flour, cinnamon, allspice, ginger, cloves, cardamom, pepper, baking powder, and salt. In a small bowl, stir together the milk and vanilla.

In the bowl of a stand mixer fitted with the paddle attachment, beat the butter and sugar on medium-high speed until light and fluffy, 2 to 3 minutes. Reduce the speed to medium-low, add the eggs one at a time, and beat until creamy, 1 to 2 minutes. Slowly add half the flour mixture, then the milk mixture, then the remaining flour mixture, beating until just blended after each addition.

Divide the batter evenly among the liners and bake until the tops are just dry to the touch and a toothpick inserted into the center comes out clean, 17 to 19 minutes. Transfer the pan to a wire rack and cool completely before frosting with chai latte frosting.

✳ To bake as a cake, see the box on page 16.

CHAI LATTE FROSTING

MAKES 2 CUPS

3 cups confectioners' sugar

¼ teaspoon ground cinnamon

¼ teaspoon ground allspice

¼ teaspoon ground ginger

¼ teaspoon ground cardamom

Large pinch of ground cloves

Large pinch of freshly ground black pepper

¼ teaspoon fine sea salt

1 cup (2 sticks) unsalted butter, slightly softened

1 tablespoon whole milk

¼ teaspoon pure vanilla extract

In a medium bowl, sift together the confectioners' sugar, cinnamon, allspice, ginger, cardamom, cloves, pepper, and salt.

In the bowl of a stand mixer fitted with the paddle attachment, beat the butter on medium-high speed until creamy, 2 minutes. Reduce the speed to low and gradually add the confectioners' sugar mixture, milk, and vanilla and beat until blended, being careful not to incorporate too much air into the frosting.

THE BARBRA STREISAND CUPCAKE

MAKES 12 CUPCAKES

I will never forget meeting Barbra Streisand for the first time at an Academy Awards party. Barbra was an icon. Barbra was a legend. And Barbra was…a Sprinkles customer! I knew she loved our cupcakes, but I wasn't prepared for her depth of knowledge when it came to food. And when she began talking about specific dessert techniques from *Joy of Cooking* recipes, I was equally blown away by her passion for baking. She told me how much she loved our vanilla cupcakes, and asked us to create a thin chocolate ganache glaze reminiscent of one she made at home using a melted semisweet chocolate bar. This became a special "off the menu" flavor we made only when Barbra called. Barbra was also instrumental in introducing us to Oprah Winfrey. Not long after we opened, she had a dozen Sprinkles Cupcakes delivered to Oprah in Santa Barbara. Soon after, Oprah invited us to be on her show. Once the episode aired, we had lines around the block that seemed to never end. We sent Barbra a picture of that winding customer line, inscribed with a quote from Oprah herself: "Look at what you started!" Thank you a million times over, Barbra.

1½ **cups all-purpose flour**	½ **cup (1 stick) unsalted butter, slightly softened**
1 **teaspoon baking powder**	
¼ **teaspoon baking soda**	1 **cup sugar**
¼ **teaspoon fine sea salt**	1 **large egg**
⅔ **cup whole milk**	2 **large egg whites**
1½ **teaspoons pure vanilla extract**	**Chocolate Ganache (page 49)**

Preheat the oven to 325°F. Line a 12-cup cupcake pan with paper liners.

In a medium bowl, whisk together the flour, baking powder, baking soda, and salt. In a small bowl, stir together the milk and vanilla.

In the bowl of a stand mixer fitted with the paddle attachment, beat the butter and sugar on medium-high speed until light and fluffy, 2 to 3 minutes. Reduce the speed to medium-low, add the egg and egg whites one at a time, and beat until creamy, 1 to 2 minutes. Slowly add half the flour mixture, then the milk mixture, then the remaining flour mixture, beating until just blended after each addition.

Divide the batter evenly among the liners and bake until the tops are just dry to the touch and a toothpick inserted into the center comes out clean, 18 to 20 minutes. Transfer the pan to a wire rack and cool completely.

Dunk the top of each cupcake into the ganache and quickly turn right-side up, cleaning any drips from the side. Allow the cupcakes to set at room temperature for 30 to 45 minutes. If desired, dunk the tops in ganache a second time for extra coverage (I highly recommend this!) and let set until dry.

CHOCOLATE CHIP COOKIE CUPCAKES

MAKES 12 CUPCAKES

You know I'm a fan of a great mash-up, and since Sprinkles is famous for its ice cream cupcake mash-ups, why not a cookie cupcake mash-up? Here, I take two of my favorite things in the world—cupcakes and chocolate chip cookies—and make them one. This is a case where the sum truly is greater than its parts: crunchy chocolate chip cookie crumbs become a crisp crust for a chocolate chip cupcake to sit upon, and the brown sugar frosting is reminiscent of chocolate chip cookie dough. Heaven!

FOR THE COOKIE CRUST[*]:

Half recipe of Thin & Crispy Chocolate Chip Cookie "Monsters" (p. 116)

1½ teaspoons unsalted butter, melted

[*] If you're short on time, you can replace the homemade cookies with 12 crisp supermarket-style chocolate chip cookies (such as Chips Ahoy!) or 6 gourmet-style chocolate chip cookies (such as Tate's); the rest of the recipe for the crust remains the same.

FOR THE CUPCAKES:

1½ cups all-purpose flour

1 teaspoon baking powder

¼ teaspoon baking soda

¼ teaspoon fine sea salt

⅔ cup whole milk

1½ teaspoons pure vanilla extract

½ cup (1 stick) unsalted butter, slightly softened

1 cup sugar

2 large eggs

¾ cup semisweet chocolate chips

Cookie Dough Frosting

MAKE THE COOKIE CRUST:

Preheat the oven to 350°F. Line a 12-cup cupcake pan with paper liners.

Place the cookies in a food processor and process into fine crumbs, then transfer to a bowl. Add the melted butter and 1 teaspoon water and stir well with a fork. Scoop 1 tablespoon of the crumb mixture into each liner and press down firmly with the back of the spoon to create an even layer. Bake for 5 minutes, then transfer to a wire rack to cool completely. Reduce the oven temperature to 325°F.

COOKIE DOUGH FROSTING

MAKES 1¾ CUPS

⅓ cup lightly packed light brown sugar

1 tablespoon whole milk

½ teaspoon pure vanilla extract

¾ cup (1½ sticks) unsalted butter, slightly softened

¼ teaspoon fine sea salt

1¾ cups confectioners' sugar, sifted

In a medium saucepan, heat the brown sugar and milk over medium-low heat until the sugar has dissolved, 2 minutes. Remove from the heat and cool to room temperature. Stir in the vanilla.

In the bowl of a stand mixer fitted with the paddle attachment, beat the butter, brown sugar mixture, and salt until light and fluffy. Reduce the speed to low, gradually add the confectioners' sugar, and beat until just incorporated.

MAKE THE CUPCAKES:

In a medium bowl, whisk together the flour, baking powder, baking soda, and salt. In a small bowl, stir together the milk and vanilla.

In the bowl of a stand mixer fitted with the paddle attachment, beat the butter and sugar on medium-high speed until light and fluffy, 2 to 3 minutes. Reduce the speed to medium-low, add the eggs one at a time, and beat until creamy, 1 to 2 minutes. Slowly add half the flour mixture, then the milk mixture, then the remaining flour mixture, beating until just blended after each addition. Stir in chocolate chips by hand.

Divide the batter evenly among the crust-lined cupcake liners and bake until the tops are just dry to the touch and a toothpick inserted into the center comes out clean, 18 to 20 minutes. Transfer the pan to a wire rack and cool completely before frosting with cookie dough frosting.

WHEN OPRAH CALLS

Nine months after opening our Beverly Hills bakery, I received a call from Oprah Winfrey's producers at Harpo Studios in Chicago. Apparently, Barbra Streisand had delivered Oprah a box of our cupcakes, and Oprah had given them her illustrious—and potentially life-changing—seal of approval. They asked if we wanted to provide cupcakes for the studio audience of an Oprah taping . . . the only catch being that they needed them the next morning! I answered with an emphatic yes, realizing before I even hung up that I had no idea how we were going to get four hundred fragile little cupcakes to Chicago in little more than twelve hours. That same night, Charles and I boarded a red-eye, hand-carrying every last one of those precious cupcake babies ourselves. When the TSA agents heard "We're going to Oprah!" even they eased up as we loaded box after box through the X-ray conveyor belt. On the journey, flight attendants and fellow passengers were giving us high-fives; everyone was rooting for us. The show aired, the cupcakes were a hit, and overnight, Sprinkles became a brand known around the world. Never underestimate the power of Oprah!

STRAWBERRY CHEESECAKE CUPCAKES

MAKES 12 CUPCAKES

This cupcake originated as an off-the-menu flavor, successfully harnessing the slightly savory crunch of our graham cracker crust to balance the sweetness of the strawberry cake and tangy cream cheese frosting. Because strawberries are difficult to use in baked goods due to their high water content, most strawberry cakes call for artificial flavoring. My cake, however, uses sweet pureed strawberries to deliver a delicate yet tantalizing fruit flavor. In 2015, we partnered with singer Ne-Yo to sell this new flavor to benefit his charity, the Compound Foundation.

FOR THE GRAHAM CRUSTS:

7 whole graham crackers (14 squares)

2½ tablespoons unsalted butter, melted

FOR THE CUPCAKES:

1½ cups all-purpose flour, sifted

1 teaspoon baking powder

¼ teaspoon fine sea salt

¾ cup whole hulled fresh or frozen strawberries (thawed if frozen)

¼ cup whole milk, at room temperature

1 teaspoon pure vanilla extract

½ cup (1 stick) unsalted butter, slightly softened

1 cup sugar

1 large egg, at room temperature

2 large egg whites, at room temperature

Cream Cheese Frosting (page 14)

MAKE THE GRAHAM CRUSTS:

Preheat the oven to 350°F. Line a 12-cup cupcake pan with paper liners.

In a food processor, process the graham crackers into fine crumbs. Transfer to a bowl and stir in the melted butter until coated. Scoop 1 tablespoon of the crumb mixture into each cupcake liner and press down firmly with the back of the spoon to create an even layer. Bake until the crust slightly pulls away from the sides of the cupcake liners but is still a bit crumbly and soft when gently pressed, 7 minutes. Transfer the pan to a wire rack and cool completely. Keep the oven on.

MAKE THE CUPCAKES:

In a medium bowl, whisk together the flour, baking powder, and salt.

In a food processor (or mini chopper), puree the strawberries until smooth. Transfer to a small bowl and whisk in the milk and vanilla.

In the bowl of a stand mixer fitted with the paddle attachment, beat the butter and sugar on medium-high speed until light and fluffy, 2 to 3 minutes. Reduce the speed to medium-low, add the egg and egg whites one at a time, and beat until creamy, 1 to 2 minutes. Slowly add half the flour mixture, then the milk mixture, then the remaining flour mixture, beating until just blended after each addition.

Divide the batter evenly among the crust-lined liners and bake until the tops are just dry to the touch and a toothpick inserted into the center comes out clean, 21 to 23 minutes. Transfer the pan to a wire rack and cool completely before frosting with cream cheese frosting.

FLOURLESS CHOCOLATE CUPCAKES

MAKES 12 CUPCAKES

Long before the gluten-free trend took off, Sprinkles offered this sinful flourless chocolate cupcake for our customers who were steering clear of flour. Little more than bittersweet chocolate blended with eggs and butter, this cupcake possesses a rich flavor and luxurious mouthfeel that clearly wants for nothing! And for those tired of chocolate-covered matzo, this cake is perfect for Passover, too! At the store, we top it with a vanilla bean glaze, but I actually prefer it with slightly sweetened crème fraîche–enriched whipped cream that showcases the cupcake's intensity even more.

1 cup (2 sticks) unsalted butter, plus more for greasing

2 ounces bittersweet chocolate, chopped

4 large eggs, beaten

¾ cup sugar

½ cup lightly packed light brown sugar

1 cup unsweetened cocoa powder

2 teaspoons pure vanilla extract

1 tablespoon strong prepared espresso or coffee

½ teaspoon fine sea salt

FOR THE CRÈME FRAÎCHE CREAM:

⅔ cup heavy cream

2 tablespoons sugar

1 vanilla bean, halved lengthwise and seeds scraped, or 2 teaspoons pure vanilla extract

⅓ cup crème fraîche

MAKE THE CREAM:

In the bowl of a stand mixer fitted with the whisk attachment, whip the cream, sugar, and vanilla until soft peaks form, 2 minutes. Add the crème fraîche and beat for 30 seconds more, until the cream is billowy.

Top each cupcake with about 2 tablespoons of the crème fraîche cream.

Preheat the oven to 375°F. Generously butter an unlined 12-cup cupcake pan.

In a medium microwave-safe bowl, microwave the chocolate and butter on high for 2 to 3 minutes, stopping and stirring every 45 seconds until melted. Let the mixture cool for 5 minutes, then whisk in the eggs. Add both sugars and whisk until smooth. Add half the cocoa powder, then the vanilla and coffee, then the remaining cocoa and salt, stirring until just combined after each addition.

Divide the batter evenly among the wells of the prepared pan and bake until the tops of the cupcakes are just set, 15 to 17 minutes. Transfer the pan to a wire rack and cool completely (the centers will sink and crack slightly).

CRÈME BRÛLÉE CUPCAKES

MAKES 12 CUPCAKES

One thing I adore about cupcakes is their versatility. Here, a ramekin stands in for the traditional cupcake wrapper, transforming a hand-held treat into a dessert worthy of a dinner party. The addition of a crème brûlée topping to a vanilla cupcake makes two old familiar desserts fresh and new again. Right before serving, broil or torch the top to get that signature crispy shell; breaking through the golden caramel to get to the silky vanilla bean custard and fluffy cake is as thrilling as it is delicious. I use a fresh vanilla bean here, which adds an extra-special touch to the pastry cream, but you can always replace it with 2 teaspoons pure vanilla extract.

FOR THE PASTRY CREAM:

1 cup heavy cream

⅔ cup whole milk

6 tablespoons plus 2 tablespoons sugar

⅛ teaspoon fine sea salt

½ vanilla bean, halved lengthwise and seeds scraped, or 2 teaspoons pure vanilla extract

4 large egg yolks

3 tablespoons cornstarch

1 tablespoon unsalted butter

FOR THE CUPCAKES AND TOPPING:

1⅔ cups all-purpose flour

1¼ teaspoons baking powder

½ teaspoon fine sea salt

⅔ cup whole milk

2 teaspoons pure vanilla extract

10 tablespoons (1¼ sticks) unsalted butter, slightly softened, plus more for greasing

¾ cup plus 6 tablespoons sugar

2 large eggs

1 egg white

TIP: VANILLA SUGAR

Many of my recipes call for the interior of a vanilla bean, which lends a rich, floral vanilla flavor. After scraping the pod, you're left with the shell, and it's a shame to waste it. Simply place one or two scraped vanilla beans in a 2-cup glass container with a tight-fitting lid, fill the container with sugar, close tightly, and wait 2 weeks. When you open the container, the scent of vanilla will permeate the air—and your desserts. Use it wherever sugar is called for.

MAKE THE PASTRY CREAM:

In a medium saucepan, combine the heavy cream, milk, 6 tablespoons of the sugar, the salt, and the vanilla bean seeds and pod and bring to a low simmer over medium-low heat, stirring occasionally and removing from the heat occasionally to prevent vigorous boiling, if necessary. In a small bowl, whisk together the egg yolks and the remaining 2 tablespoons of sugar until well blended. Whisk the cornstarch into the egg mixture until slightly pale and fluffy.

Temper the egg yolk mixture by slowly pouring about ½ cup of the hot cream mixture into the eggs in a thin stream while whisking continuously. Reduce the heat to medium-low, then slowly add the egg yolk mixture into the hot cream mixture in a steady stream. Cook, whisking continuously, until thickened, then boil for 30 seconds to eliminate any starchiness. Using a silicone spatula or wooden spoon, immediately push the mixture through a fine-mesh strainer into a bowl, then whisk in the butter until smooth. Cover with plastic wrap, pressing it directly against the surface of the custard to prevent a skin from forming, and chill thoroughly, about 2 hours.

MAKE THE CUPCAKES:

Preheat the oven to 350°F. Butter twelve 4-ounce ramekins (the ramekins should measure about 3 inches in diameter) and place on a baking sheet. (If you don't have ramekins, any oven-safe 4-ounce bowls will work, or line a 12-cup cupcake pan with paper liners.)

In a medium bowl, whisk together the flour, baking powder, and salt. In a small bowl, stir together the milk and vanilla.

In the bowl of a stand mixer fitted with the paddle attachment, beat the butter and ¾ cup of the sugar on medium-high speed until light and fluffy, 2 to 3 minutes. Reduce the speed to medium-low, add the eggs and egg white one at a time, and beat until creamy, 1 to 2 minutes. Slowly add half the flour mixture, then the milk mixture, then the remaining flour mixture, beating until just blended after each addition.

Divide the batter evenly among the ramekins or liners, filling each with about ¼ cup of the batter. Bake until the tops are just dry to the touch and a toothpick inserted into the center comes out clean, 16 to 18 minutes. Carefully transfer the pan to a wire rack and cool completely.

FILL AND ASSEMBLE THE CUPCAKES:

Using a small, sharp knife, cut a circle in the center of the cupcake to create a deep hole about 1 inch in diameter. Fill each cupcake with 2 teaspoons of the pastry cream.* Using an offset spatula, spread an additional teaspoon of pastry cream over the top of each cupcake in an even layer. One cupcake at a time, evenly sprinkle 1½ teaspoons of sugar on top of each cupcake. Using a brûlée torch, torch the cupcakes until the sugar begins to melt and caramelize, 1 to 2 minutes.** If baking in cupcake liners, be extra cautious of burning the paper. Allow the topping to cool, then serve right away.

* The pastry cream can be made the day before and the cupcakes can be made hours ahead of time, but top with sugar and caramelize just before serving.

** To use your broiler to caramelize the cupcake tops, preheat the broiler, then place the sugared cupcakes on a rimmed baking sheet and broil until golden and caramelized, 1 to 2 minutes, checking often to prevent burning.

PINEAPPLE UPSIDE-DOWN CUPCAKES

MAKES 12 CUPCAKES

A classic pineapple upside-down cake can be a little tricky; getting the brown sugar to melt evenly and inverting the cake in one smooth motion can sometimes be nerve-racking. But in cupcake form, the pineapple always seems to caramelize to perfection, and if you use a nonstick cupcake pan, the process of making these gorgeous, golden individual cakes seems a little more manageable—with results that are pretty spot-on every time. The secret is to use the perfect ratio of butter to brown sugar, which helps affix the juicy pineapple to the moist, molasses-enriched cakes. Then allow the cupcakes to cool slightly, but not all the way; while still warm, they pop out of the pan with ease.

FOR THE BATTER:

1½ cups all-purpose flour

1½ teaspoons baking soda

¼ teaspoon fine sea salt

¾ cup whole milk

3 tablespoons molasses

1 tablespoon pure vanilla extract

½ cup (1 stick) unsalted butter, slightly softened

1 cup lightly packed dark brown sugar

2 large eggs

FOR THE PINEAPPLE UPSIDE-DOWN TOPPING:

Butter for greasing

6 tablespoons lightly packed dark brown sugar

4 tablespoons (½ stick) unsalted butter, melted

1 (4-ounce) piece ripe pineapple, or 6 juice-packed canned pineapple rings

Sweet Whipped Cream if desired

MAKE THE BATTER:

Preheat the oven to 350°F.

In a medium bowl, whisk together the flour, baking soda, and salt. In a small bowl, stir together the milk, molasses, and vanilla.

In the bowl of a stand mixer fitted with the paddle attachment, beat the butter and brown sugar on medium-high speed until light and fluffy, 2 to 3 minutes. Reduce the speed to medium-low, add the eggs one at a time, and beat until creamy, 1 to 2 minutes. Slowly add half the flour mixture, then the milk mixture, then the remaining flour mixture, beating until just blended after each addition.

SWEET WHIPPED CREAM

MAKES 2 CUPS

Based on the recipe we use in our ice cream shops, this perfect topping is the essence of indulgence; sweet cream, whipped with just a hint of vanilla, is versatile and very, very irresistible.

1 cup heavy cream

3 tablespoons confectioners' sugar

½ teaspoon pure vanilla extract

In the chilled bowl of a stand mixer fitted with the whisk attachment, or in a large bowl using a handheld mixer, whip the cream, confectioners' sugar, and vanilla until soft peaks form, 2 minutes. Cover and chill until ready to use.

ARRANGE THE TOPPING AND BAKE THE CUPCAKES:

Generously butter an unlined 12-cup cupcake pan. Sprinkle 1½ teaspoons of the brown sugar on the bottom of each well, then drizzle 1 teaspoon of the melted butter on top of the sugar. If using fresh pineapple, slice the pineapple into 1-inch-square, ⅛-inch-thick pieces and arrange three pieces, slightly overlapping, in the bottom of each well. (If using canned pineapple, pat the pineapple rings dry with paper towels. Cut each ring in half, then cut each half into three equal-size pieces. Arrange the three pieces in the bottom of each well.)

Divide the batter evenly among the wells and bake until the tops are puffy and dry to the touch and a toothpick inserted into the center comes out clean, 17 to 19 minutes. Transfer to a wire rack and cool for 25 to 30 minutes, then invert onto a baking sheet so the pineapple is on top. (If you don't get to invert within 30 minutes, fill a rimmed baking sheet with hot water and set the cupcake pan in the water for 1 minute to loosen the cupcakes, then invert.) Serve with sweet whipped cream, if desired.

CHAPTER 4

SEASONAL CUPCAKES

In Los Angeles, where I live, I can't always tell what time of year it is by looking outside, so I rely on the aromas emanating from the bakery to give me clues. It's a fun, edible reminder that there is truly a cupcake for every season! Cranberry-scented with orange for Thanksgiving, minty chocolate leading up to Christmas, fresh key limes to celebrate summer—these are just a few of the cupcakes that have become my calendar!

I love using fresh, seasonal ingredients in my baking, and this is one chapter where they really shine. However, most of the ingredients can be found year-round, meaning that if you must have a summery cupcake fix while hibernating through a cold winter, you're no more than a recipe away . . .

BROWN SUGAR PRALINE CUPCAKES

MAKES 12 CUPCAKES OR ONE 2-LAYER 9-INCH CAKE

Some Sprinkles flavors are seasonal, either because they are associated with certain holidays or because we like to keep the in-store flavor rotation fresh and exciting. That being said, fans of certain varieties will go to great lengths for their favorites. I will never forget the savvy customer who arrived on the last day of our brown sugar praline cupcake's annual run—and literally bought us out. She told us she was headed straight home to freeze every last one of them so she could make them last for months to come. All I can say is, well played! For those of you who've tried the flavor in-store but can't wait all year for our brown sugar praline to return—or who simply don't have the freezer space—here's the recipe. Using both molasses and dark brown sugar results in a gloriously deep, complex flavor. While the in-store cupcake comes with a candied praline topping, the home version's simple, ground pecan topping tempers the frosting's sweetness beautifully.

1½ cups all-purpose flour

1½ teaspoons baking soda

¼ teaspoon fine sea salt

¾ cup whole milk

3 tablespoons molasses

1 tablespoon pure vanilla extract

½ cup (1 stick) unsalted butter, slightly softened

1 cup lightly packed dark brown sugar

2 large eggs

Brown Sugar Frosting

¾ cup pecan halves, for topping

Preheat the oven to 350°F. Line a 12-cup cupcake pan with paper liners.

In a medium bowl, whisk together the flour, baking soda, and salt. In a small bowl, stir together the milk, molasses, and vanilla.

In the bowl of a stand mixer fitted with the paddle attachment, beat the butter and brown sugar on medium-high speed until light and fluffy, 2 to 3 minutes. Reduce the speed to medium-low, add the eggs one at a time, and beat until creamy, 1 to 2 minutes. Slowly add half the flour mixture, then the milk mixture, then the remaining flour mixture, beating until just blended after each addition. (The batter may appear slightly separated; this is okay.)

BROWN SUGAR FROSTING

MAKES 2 CUPS

½ cup (1 stick) unsalted butter

1 cup lightly packed light brown sugar

¼ cup whole milk, plus more as needed

1½ cups confectioners' sugar, sifted

In a medium saucepan, heat the butter and brown sugar together over medium heat, stirring, until the brown sugar has dissolved, 1 to 2 minutes. Bring the mixture to a boil, then reduce the heat to low and simmer, stirring continuously, for 2 minutes. Add the milk and return to a boil, stirring continuously, until the mixture is well combined, 2 minutes. Remove from the heat and cool to lukewarm, 20 minutes. While whisking continuously, gradually add the confectioners' sugar. Add additional milk 1 tablespoon at a time if the frosting becomes too stiff (it should be firm but still spreadable).

Divide the batter evenly among the liners and bake until the tops are puffy and dry to the touch and a toothpick inserted into the center comes out clean, 16 to 18 minutes. Transfer the pan to a wire rack and cool completely.

While the cupcakes are cooling, in a heavy-bottomed skillet, toast the pecans over medium-low heat, stirring frequently, for 7 to 8 minutes. Transfer to a plate to cool. Once cool, place in a food processor and process until the nuts are the size of large bread crumbs, 10 to 15 seconds. Frost the cupcakes with brown sugar frosting and arrange them on a baking sheet. Sprinkle the toasted pecan crumbs evenly over the cupcakes, gently pressing to adhere them to the frosting and letting excess pecan crumbs fall onto the baking sheet.

* To bake as a cake, See the box on page 16. Sprinkle some pecan crumbs in between the two layers and pile the rest of the crumbs on top.

KEY LIME PIE CUPCAKES

MAKES 12 CUPCAKES

You know it's summer in the Sprinkles bakery kitchen when you smell the aroma of key limes; if you closed your eyes, you might think you were on a tropical island! Our bakers grate mounds and mounds of tiny key limes for their exquisitely fragrant rinds, then squeeze out every last drop of their precious, elusive juice. Key lime season officially begins in June, but it may take until late summer to see them in grocery stores, so snatch them up for use in this creamy, crunchy, lip-puckering palate pleaser. Here's a pro tip to help extract as much juice as possible: microwave the limes for 15 to 30 seconds, then roll them against the countertop with the palm of your hand before slicing and squeezing; a pointy-ended citrus reamer is the ideal tool for the job.

FOR THE LIME CURD:

3 large egg yolks

¾ cup plus 1½ tablespoons sugar

3 tablespoons cornstarch

⅛ teaspoon fine sea salt

¾ cup cold water

6 tablespoons half-and-half

1½ tablespoons unsalted butter

1½ tablespoons finely grated, lightly packed key lime zest, or zest of 2 regular limes

¼ cup fresh key lime juice or regular fresh lime juice

FOR THE GRAHAM CRUSTS:

7 whole graham crackers (14 squares)

2½ tablespoons unsalted butter, melted

FOR THE CUPCAKES:

1½ cups all-purpose flour

1 teaspoon baking powder

¼ teaspoon baking soda

¼ teaspoon fine sea salt

⅔ cup whole milk

2 tablespoons lightly packed key lime zest, or zest of 3 regular limes

½ teaspoon pure vanilla extract

½ cup (1 stick) unsalted butter, slightly softened

1 cup sugar

1 large egg

2 large egg whites

Marshmallow Frosting (page 49), for frosting

MAKE THE LIME CURD:

In a medium bowl, whisk the egg yolks. In a nonreactive medium saucepan, whisk together the sugar, cornstarch, and salt. Stir in the water and half-and-half and cook over medium heat, stirring frequently, until the mixture just starts to boil, 5 to 6 minutes. Temper

the egg yolks by whisking in a few tablespoons of the hot sugar mixture, 1 tablespoon at a time, then slowly add the tempered yolks back to the sugar mixture in the saucepan, whisking briskly. Cook over medium-low heat, whisking continuously, until the mixture returns to a boil and large bubbles form on the surface, 3 minutes; the surface should be thick and glossy like pudding. Remove from the heat and strain through a fine-mesh sieve into a bowl. Stir in the butter until melted completely, then stir in the lime zest and juice; cool slightly, then cover with plastic wrap, pressing it directly against the surface of the curd to prevent a skin from forming, and chill until ready to use.

MAKE THE GRAHAM CRUSTS:

Preheat the oven to 350°F. Line a 12-cup cupcake pan with paper liners. In a food processor, process the graham crackers into fine crumbs. Transfer to a bowl and stir in the melted butter until coated. Scoop 1 tablespoon of the crumb mixture into each cupcake liner and press down firmly with the back of the spoon to create an even layer. Bake until the crust slightly pulls away from the sides of the cupcake liners but is still a bit crumbly and soft when gently pressed, 7 minutes. Remove from the oven and let cool. Keep the oven on.

MAKE THE CUPCAKES:

In a medium bowl, whisk together the flour, baking powder, baking soda, and salt. In a small saucepan, heat the milk and lime zest over low heat until hot but not boiling, 3 minutes; cool until lukewarm, 5 minutes, then stir in the vanilla.

In the bowl of a stand mixer fitted with the paddle attachment, beat the butter and sugar on medium-high speed until light and fluffy, 2 to 3 minutes. Reduce the speed to medium-low, add the egg and egg whites one at a time, and beat until creamy, 1 to 2 minutes. Slowly add half the flour mixture, then the milk mixture, then the remaining flour mixture, beating until just blended after each addition. Divide the batter evenly among the liners and bake until the tops are just dry to the touch (some may be slightly golden on the sides before this happens) and a toothpick inserted into the center comes out clean, 18 to 20 minutes.

FILL AND FINISH THE CUPCAKES:

Using a small, sharp knife, cut a circle into the center of each cupcake to create a hole about 1½ inches wide and 1 inch deep (reserve the scoops for snacking!), making sure not to dig too deep into the cupcake so the filling does not leak out the bottom. Fill each cupcake with 1½ tablespoons of the curd (you may have a couple of tablespoons remaining; enjoy!). Frost with the marshmallow frosting and brown with a brûlée torch, if desired. Or, to use your broiler to caramelize the cupcake tops, preheat the broiler, then place the cupcakes on a rimmed baking sheet and broil until golden, about 1 minute, watching the entire time to ensure that they don't burn.

LEMON BLUEBERRY CUPCAKES

MAKES 12 CUPCAKES OR ONE 2-LAYER 9-INCH CAKE

When I was a girl, few things compared to a family outing to a "u-pick" blueberry farm. Filling a bucket with, and snacking on, those tart berries gave me an early window into just how delicious juicy, sun-ripened fruit could be. Though the fruits of my labor were typically baked into a blueberry pie, they would have been equally welcome as an ingredient in these cupcakes, which burst with the bright, tangy essence of fresh lemons and pop with juicy blueberries. At our stores, this variety often stands in as a quick breakfast among the staff. In a bit of delicious self-deception, we tell ourselves that without the frosting, it's just like a muffin. Don't spoil it for us!

1½ cups plus 1 tablespoon all-purpose flour

1 teaspoon baking powder

¼ teaspoon baking soda

¼ teaspoon fine sea salt

1 cup fresh blueberries

⅔ cup whole milk

2 tablespoons finely grated, lightly packed lemon zest (from 3 medium lemons)

½ teaspoon pure vanilla extract

½ cup (1 stick) unsalted butter, slightly softened

1 cup sugar

1 large egg

2 large egg whites

Lemon Frosting

Preheat the oven to 325°F. Line a 12-cup cupcake pan with paper liners.

In a medium bowl, whisk together 1½ cups of the flour, the baking powder, baking soda, and salt. In a small bowl, toss the blueberries with the remaining 1 tablespoon flour.

In a small saucepan, heat the milk and lemon zest over low heat until hot but not boiling, 3 to 4 minutes. Remove from the heat and cool until lukewarm; stir in the vanilla.

In the bowl of a stand mixer fitted with the paddle attachment, beat the butter and sugar on medium-high speed until light and fluffy, 2 to 3 minutes. Reduce the speed to medium-low, add the egg and egg whites one at a time, and beat until creamy, 1 to 2 minutes. Slowly add half the flour mixture, then the milk mixture, then the remaining flour mixture, beating until just blended after each addition. Using a silicone spatula, gently fold in the blueberries.

LEMON FROSTING

MAKES 2 CUPS

1 cup (2 sticks) unsalted butter, slightly softened

⅛ teaspoon fine sea salt

3 cups confectioners' sugar, sifted

1 teaspoon whole milk

1 tablespoon finely grated lemon zest (from 1 medium lemon)

1 tablespoon fresh lemon juice

⅛ teaspoon pure vanilla extract

In the bowl of a stand mixer fitted with the paddle attachment, beat the butter and salt on medium speed until light and fluffy, 2 to 3 minutes. Reduce the speed to low, gradually add the confectioners' sugar, and beat until incorporated. Increase the speed to medium, add the milk, lemon zest and juice, and vanilla, and beat until fully blended, 1 to 2 minutes, making sure not to incorporate too much air into the frosting.

Divide the batter evenly among the liners and bake until the tops are just dry to the touch and a toothpick inserted into the center comes out clean (some may be slightly golden on the sides before this happens), 17 to 19 minutes. Transfer the pan to a wire rack and cool completely before frosting with lemon frosting.

✳ To bake as a cake, see the box on page 16.

BLAKE LIVELY'S S'MORE CUPCAKES

MAKES 12 CUPCAKES

Sprinkles couldn't have asked for a more perfect first charitable ambassador than the lovely Blake Lively. Not only has she been vocal on the red carpet about her love for our cupcakes, she's a passionate chef herself. She spends her time creating new treats at home; occasionally baking alongside Martha Stewart; assisting the pastry chefs at Thomas Keller's famed Per Se restaurant in New York; or being schooled by her niece, Kate, in all things confectionery. When we asked Blake to develop a flavor Sprinkles customers would love (with the proceeds raising lots of money for her charity, OXFAM), she knew exactly what she wanted to create: an experience in a bite, not just a yummy new flavor. After months of experimenting, the "grown-up" s'more cupcake was born. After all, what's more nostalgic than s'mores? For this inspired take, she created a salted graham cracker base as the foundation for a dark chocolate cake filled with chocolate ganache. The key for her, though, was the topping: how to get that campfire memory in there? Top it all off with a char-edged, toasted marshmallow frosting! It's a complete experience in a single cupcake. Our customers went crazy for it, and you will, too. The extra components require a bit more time, but if you're planning ahead, the ganache and marshmallow frosting can be made a day in advance. The memories, though—those will last a lot longer.

FOR THE CRUST:

7 whole graham crackers
(14 squares)

2½ tablespoons unsalted butter, melted

FOR THE CUPCAKES:

1 cup all-purpose flour

⅔ cup unsweetened cocoa powder

¾ teaspoon baking powder

½ teaspoon baking soda

½ teaspoon fine sea salt

⅔ cup buttermilk, shaken

1 teaspoon pure vanilla extract

10 tablespoons (1¼ sticks) unsalted butter, slightly softened

⅔ cup sugar

⅓ cup lightly packed light brown sugar

2 large eggs

FOR THE GANACHE:

Chocolate Ganache Frosting
(page 49)

Marshmallow Frosting (page 49)

(Continued)

MAKE THE CRUST:

Preheat the oven to 350°F. Line a 12-cup cupcake pan with paper liners.

In a food processor, process the graham crackers into fine crumbs. Transfer to a bowl and stir in the melted butter until coated. Scoop 1 tablespoon of crumb mixture into each cupcake liner and press down firmly with the back of the spoon to create an even layer. Bake until the crust slightly pulls away from the sides of the cupcake liners but is still a bit crumbly and soft when gently pressed, 7 minutes. Transfer the pan to a wire rack and cool completely. Keep the oven on.

MAKE THE CUPCAKES:

In a medium bowl, whisk together the flour, cocoa powder, baking powder, baking soda, and salt. In a small bowl, stir together the buttermilk and vanilla.

In the bowl of a stand mixer fitted with the paddle attachment, beat the butter and both sugars on medium-high speed until light and fluffy, 2 to 3 minutes. Reduce the speed to medium-low, add the eggs one at a time, and beat until creamy, 1 to 2 minutes. Slowly add half the flour mixture, then the buttermilk mixture, then the remaining flour mixture, beating until just blended after each addition.

Divide the batter evenly among the crust-lined liners and bake until the tops are just dry to the touch and a toothpick inserted into the center comes out clean, 18 to 20 minutes. Transfer the pan to a wire rack and cool completely.

FILL AND TOP THE CUPCAKES:

Using a sharp knife, cut a circle into the center of the cupcake to create a hole about 1½ inches wide and 1 inch deep (reserve the scoops for snacking!), making sure not to dig too deep into the cupcake so the filling does not leak out the bottom. Fill each cupcake with 1½ tablespoons of the ganache, then allow the ganache to set for 10 to 15 minutes. Frost with marshmallow frosting and toast with a brûlée torch, if desired. Or, to use your broiler to brown the cupcake tops, preheat the broiler, then place the cupcakes on a rimmed baking sheet and broil until golden, about 1 minute, watching the entire time to ensure they don't burn.

ORANGE CRANBERRY CUPCAKES

MAKES 12 CUPCAKES OR ONE 2-LAYER 9-INCH CAKE

Though cupcakes haven't traditionally been a Thanksgiving dessert in this country, I like to think Sprinkles has had a hand in changing that. Every November, Sprinkles offers its extraordinarily popular EAT box, which includes a variety of cupcakes—including these orange cranberry delights. The sweet, fresh flavor of orange, studded with tart cranberries (fresh and frozen work equally well), makes for a vibrant dessert as worthy of Thanksgiving as any pie.

1½ cups plus 1 tablespoon all-purpose flour

1 teaspoon baking powder

¼ teaspoon baking soda

¼ teaspoon fine sea salt

⅔ cup whole milk

2 tablespoons lightly packed finely grated orange zest (from 2 large oranges)

½ teaspoon pure vanilla extract

½ cup (1 stick) unsalted butter, slightly softened

1 cup sugar

1 large egg

2 large egg whites

1 cup fresh or unthawed frozen cranberries

Orange Frosting

Preheat the oven to 325°F. Line a 12-cup cupcake pan with paper liners.

In a medium bowl, whisk together 1½ cups of the flour, the baking powder, baking soda, and salt. In a small saucepan, heat the milk and orange zest over low heat until hot (but not boiling); cool to lukewarm, 4 to 5 minutes. Stir in the vanilla.

In the bowl of a stand mixer fitted with the paddle attachment, beat the butter and sugar on medium-high speed until light and fluffy, 2 to 3 minutes. Reduce the speed to medium-low, add the egg and egg whites one at a time, and beat until creamy, 1 to 2 minutes. Slowly add half the flour mixture, then the milk mixture, then the remaining flour mixture, beating until just blended after each addition. In a small bowl, toss the cranberries with the remaining 1 tablespoon flour. Using a silicone spatula, gently fold the cranberries into the batter.

Divide the batter evenly among the liners and bake until the tops are just dry to the touch (some may be slightly golden on the sides before this happens) and a toothpick inserted into the center comes out clean, 17 to 19 minutes. Transfer the pan to a wire rack and cool completely before frosting with orange frosting.

ORANGE FROSTING

MAKES 2 CUPS

1 cup (2 sticks) unsalted butter, slightly softened

⅛ teaspoon fine sea salt

3 cups confectioners' sugar, sifted

1 teaspoon whole milk

1 tablespoon lightly packed finely grated orange zest (from 1 large orange)

1 tablespoon fresh orange juice

⅛ teaspoon pure vanilla extract

In the bowl of a stand mixer fitted with the paddle attachment, beat the butter and salt on medium speed until light and fluffy, 2 to 3 minutes. Reduce the speed to low, gradually add the confectioners' sugar, and beat until incorporated. Increase the speed to medium, add the milk, orange zest and juice, and vanilla and beat until fully blended, 1 to 2 minutes, making sure not to incorporate too much air into the frosting.

✳ To bake as a cake, see the box on page 16.

SPICE CUPCAKES

MAKES 12 CUPCAKES OR ONE 2-LAYER 9-INCH CAKE

Even in sunny California, I still look forward to using the so-called "warm spices" that herald the start of the winter baking season. Regardless of the season, this recipe delivers a delicious dose of cozy comfort in every bite. These cupcakes combine a generous blend of cinnamon, nutmeg, ginger, and cloves into a luxurious cake sweetened with rich, dark molasses. Top them with velvety, cinnamon-laced cream cheese frosting . . . and may I suggest a latte to go along?

✳ To bake as a cake, see the box on page 16.

1½ cups all-purpose flour

½ teaspoon ground allspice

¼ teaspoon ground cinnamon

¼ teaspoon freshly grated nutmeg

¼ teaspoon ground ginger

⅛ teaspoon ground cloves

1 teaspoon baking powder

¼ teaspoon baking soda

¼ teaspoon fine sea salt

½ cup buttermilk, shaken

⅓ cup molasses

1 teaspoon pure vanilla extract

⅔ cup unsalted butter, slightly softened

⅔ cup sugar

2 large eggs

Cinnamon Cream Cheese Frosting (page 26)

Preheat the oven to 325°F. Line a 12-cup cupcake pan with paper liners.

In a medium bowl, whisk together the flour, allspice, cinnamon, nutmeg, ginger, cloves, baking powder, baking soda, and salt. In a small bowl, stir together the buttermilk, molasses, and vanilla.

In the bowl of a stand mixer fitted with the paddle attachment, beat the butter and sugar on medium-high speed until light and fluffy, 2 to 3 minutes. Reduce the speed to medium-low, add the eggs one at a time, and beat until creamy, 1 to 2 minutes. Slowly add half the flour mixture, then the buttermilk mixture, then the remaining flour mixture, beating until just blended after each addition.

Divide the batter evenly among the liners and bake until the cupcakes are dry to the touch and a toothpick inserted into the center comes out clean, 16 to 18 minutes. Transfer the pan to a wire rack and cool completely before frosting with cinnamon cream cheese frosting.

CHOCOLATE PEPPERMINT CUPCAKES

MAKES 12 CUPCAKES OR ONE 2-LAYER 9-INCH CAKE

If you love my signature Dark Chocolate Cupcakes (page 31), this seasonal play on the same flavor foundation may become your new favorite. It's got that deep, dark chocolate base, but with a fresh peppermint accent to signal that the holidays are just around the corner. The festive, crunchy peppermint candies are an extra flourish that helps these stand out on a holiday buffet—but you'll enjoy them just as much if you're curled up on the couch with a steaming mug of hot cocoa. My tip: Crush the peppermint candies or candy canes in a zip-top bag using a rolling pin. Then pick out the reddest pieces to ensure the most spirited topping!

1 cup all-purpose flour

⅔ cup unsweetened cocoa powder

¾ teaspoon baking powder

½ teaspoon baking soda

½ teaspoon fine sea salt

⅔ cup buttermilk, shaken

½ teaspoon pure vanilla extract

½ teaspoon peppermint extract

10 tablespoons (1¼ sticks) unsalted butter, slightly softened

⅔ cup sugar

⅓ cup lightly packed light brown sugar

2 large eggs

Chocolate Peppermint Frosting

20 to 24 peppermint candies, or 12 mini candy canes, lightly crushed*

Preheat the oven to 350°F. Line a 12-cup cupcake pan with paper liners.

In a medium bowl, whisk together the flour, cocoa powder, baking powder, baking soda, and salt. In a small bowl, stir together the buttermilk with the vanilla and peppermint extracts.

In the bowl of a stand mixer fitted with the paddle attachment, beat the butter and sugars on medium-high speed until light and fluffy, 2 to 3 minutes. Reduce the speed to medium-low, add the eggs one at a time, and beat until well blended, 2 minutes more. Reduce the speed to low and slowly add half the flour mixture, then the buttermilk mixture, then the remaining flour mixture, beating until just blended after each addition.

CHOCOLATE PEPPERMINT FROSTING

MAKES 2 CUPS

¾ cup (1½ sticks) unsalted butter, slightly softened

⅛ teaspoon fine sea salt

2½ cups confectioners' sugar, sifted

¼ teaspoon pure vanilla extract

½ teaspoon peppermint extract

4 ounces bittersweet chocolate, chopped, melted, and cooled to room temperature

Whole milk, if needed

In the bowl of a stand mixer fitted with the paddle attachment, beat the butter and salt on medium speed until light and fluffy, 2 minutes. Reduce the speed to low and gradually add the confectioners' sugar and the vanilla and peppermint extracts, beating until smooth and creamy. Stop the mixer and scrape down the sides of the bowl. Add the chocolate and beat on low to medium speed until incorporated, being careful not to incorporate too much air into the frosting. If necessary, add more milk 1 tablespoon at a time until the frosting has a spreadable consistency.

Divide the batter evenly among the liners and bake until the tops are just dry to the touch and a toothpick inserted into the center comes out clean, 18 to 20 minutes. Transfer the pan to a wire rack and cool completely.

Frost the cupcakes with the chocolate peppermint frosting, arrange them on a baking sheet, and sprinkle with the crushed peppermints, pressing gently to help the bits to adhere to the frosting.

* To crush the candies, place them in a zip-top bag and crush with a rolling pin into small pieces.

** To bake as a cake, see the box on page 16.

LINE 'EM UP

Cupcake liners at Sprinkles are always chocolate brown. This was a conscious decision my husband and I made when considering the cupcake display in our first store. We wanted the pretty part of the cupcake (the frosting! the decoration!) to pop, so we grounded the cake part with dark wrappers. The effect is that the whole display feels unified, and your eye is drawn to the pretty sprinkles, modern dots, and luscious frostings, not all the different cupcake liners they were baked in. We also liked the fact that the chocolate-brown wrapper helped people instantly connect our cupcakes with our brand.

At home, however, you can have fun with liners. There are endless color, and even shape, variations for every whim, party theme, and mood. One word of caution: These recipes were all baked in a standard cupcake cup, meaning that the edges of the cupcake reach all the way to the top of the cup in a full circle. Have fun with colors, but if you stray too far from this general shape and go with a scalloped edge, for example, you may not be able to divide the batter evenly without it overflowing. I have also found that if you are baking with a light-colored wrapper (like the pastel ones you find at the grocery store), it helps to double the wrappers—the first wrapper sticks to the cupcake and becomes rather translucent, while the second, which adheres well enough, adds the intended pop of color.

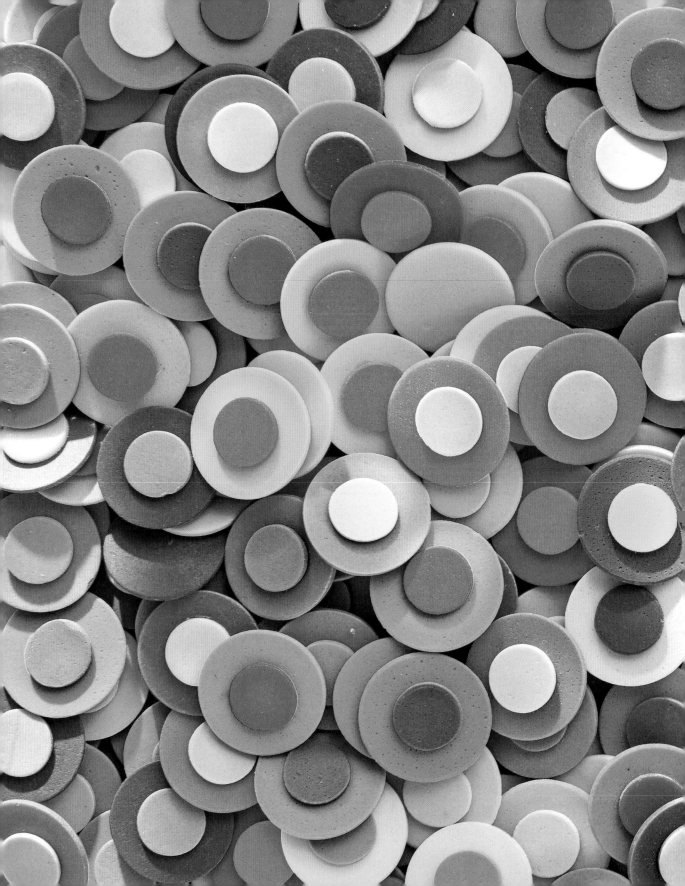

CHAPTER 5

SPRINKLES MASH-UPS

Sprinkles Cupcakes and frostings find new ways to please our customers all the time—and our customers never cease to amaze us with their creativity in transforming our desserts into novel creations! Sprinkles was literally founded on my belief in the versatility of cupcakes, and that a treat we all knew and loved as kids could be made to appeal to a much wider audience. Over the years, they've proven their adaptability even further as we worked them into countless new creations, many inspired by our loyal fans. You'll find many of them here, but this is just the tip of the icing. Who knows what we—or you—will think of next!

FROSTING SHOTS

MAKES 12 TO 14 SHOTS

If there is one thing I've learned after more than a decade in the world of cupcakes, it's that we can be divided into two camps: cake cravers and frosting fiends. For the frosting obsessed, even the generous amount we lavish atop our cupcakes leaves some hankering for more. That's why I began piping frosting into small white soufflé cups, watching in amazement as our customers snapped them up almost as quickly as we could make them. One particularly hot summer, I experimented with freezing our frosting shots. The heat wave turned into a sweet wave as these ice cream–like treats took off. Dip them in my super-easy chocolate "magic shell," add your favorite sprinkles or nuts, dust with cookie crumbs—whatever you choose, you're in for an irresistible treat.

1 recipe frosting of your choice	Jimmies or nonpareils
1 recipe Chocolate "Magic Shell"	Crushed vanilla or chocolate cookies
Finely chopped toasted peanuts or pecans	

Fit a pastry bag with a ½-inch star tip and fill the bag with the frosting (or fill a gallon-size zip-top bag with the frosting, force it into one corner, and snip a ½-inch opening from the corner). Pipe 2½ to 3 tablespoons of the frosting into 1-ounce soufflé cups, trying to make a soft serve–style peak, if possible. Arrange the filled cups on a plate or tray and freeze for 10 minutes. Sprinkle them or roll them with the topping of your choice, and return to the freezer for 20 to 30 minutes more. Serve, or keep in the freezer, loosely covered, for up to 1 day, then remove 10 minutes before serving. Alternatively, freeze the shots for 1 hour and dip in the chocolate shell. Then, working quickly, sprinkle or roll the coated shots in the topping of your choice and serve immediately.

CHOCOLATE "MAGIC SHELL"

MAKES 1¾ CUPS

I love this recipe as much for its simplicity—two ingredients!—as for the childlike wonder it evokes. Using coconut oil, which hardens on contact with cold elements, in combination with high-quality chocolate yields a more natural version of the squeeze-bottle liquid I loved as a kid.

1½ cups chopped dark chocolate

¾ cup coconut oil

In a microwave-safe bowl, microwave the chocolate and coconut oil together on high, stopping and stirring every 45 seconds, until melted and liquid, 2 to 3 minutes. Whisk briefly to emulsify the mixture. Cool to room temperature for at least 1 hour before dipping. Extra chocolate shell can be stored in the refrigerator (it will harden; gently rewarm over low heat, then cool to room temperature again before using). Save extra chocolate shell for serving on ice cream.

CUPCAKE SUNDAE

MAKES 1 SUNDAE

One of the best things about launching Sprinkles Ice Cream has been all the fun I can have combining two of my greatest dessert loves. I've always said there's no better partner for cake than ice cream, and finally I have both to play with! There are plenty of amazing ice cream concoctions on the Sprinkles Ice Cream menu, but this is the most decadent. It's nothing more than your favorite cupcake, split in half to hold your ideal scoop of ice cream, topped with whipped cream and the dessert sauce of your choice. The combinations are endless, but ooey-gooey butterscotch sauce or hot fudge are my favorites to top this towering sundae.

1 Sprinkles Cupcake of your choice

1 scoop ice cream of your choice, preferably Sprinkles

¼ cup Salted Butterscotch Sauce or Hot Fudge Sauce (page 277)

1 large dollop Sweet Whipped Cream (page 68)

Remove the wrapper from the cupcake and cut it in half horizontally, separating the top from the bottom. Add a scoop of ice cream inside the two halves and drizzle with salted butterscotch sauce or hot fudge sauce. Top with a dollop of sweet whipped cream.

SALTED BUTTERSCOTCH SAUCE

MAKES 1½ CUPS

Butterscotch is one of those old-fashioned flavors that doesn't get as much love as it deserves. Most people associate the flavor with those waxy, artificially flavored chips, but this one, made with brown sugar, heavy cream, and butter, is like a melted version of small-batch butterscotch candy. I added an extra hit of salt to update the flavor.

½ cup (1 stick) unsalted butter

1½ cups lightly packed light brown sugar

½ cup heavy cream

2 tablespoons pure vanilla extract

2½ teaspoons fine sea salt

½ teaspoon distilled white vinegar

In a medium saucepan, melt the butter over medium-high heat. Before the butter has completely melted, add the brown sugar and stir with a wooden spoon until incorporated. Increase the heat to high, bring to a boil, reduce the heat to medium and cook, stirring occasionally and making sure to stir around the edges, until the mixture first looks like grainy molten lava and then is completely smooth, 3 to 4 minutes. Whisk in the cream (mixture will bubble up slightly) and cook until incorporated, 1 minute. Remove from heat and whisk in the vanilla, salt, and vinegar. Serve warm.

CUPCAKE TOP ICE CREAM SANDWICHES

MAKES 1 ICE CREAM SANDWICH

As much as I understand the appeal of the cookie–ice cream sandwich combo (we sell them at all our Sprinkles Ice Cream shops), cookies tend to be hard, causing the ice cream to squish out the sides. Cupcake tops to the rescue! Soft and supple, they become one with the ice cream, creating the perfect sandwich bite. At Sprinkles you get to choose your favorite cupcake top and ice cream, and I love witnessing all the creative varieties our customers come up with. This couldn't be simpler: bake your favorite cupcake recipe, twist off the tops, then lay out an array of ice creams for guests to personalize their creations with your freshly baked cupcakes. Depending on the flavor you choose, the bottoms can be "recycled" for our Cupcake Truffles (page 106), Pecan Pie Cupcake Milk Shake (page 109), or Tropical Cupcake Trifle (page 102).

2 cupcake tops of your choice, preferably Sprinkles

⅓ to ½ cup ice cream flavor of your choice, slightly softened

Freeze the cupcake tops for 30 minutes to 1 hour. Place them flat-side up on a plate and scoop the ice cream into the center of one cupcake top. Close the sandwich, pressing to spread the ice cream to the edges. Eat immediately, or wrap in waxed paper and freeze for up to 1 week.

HOW TO TWIST OFF A CUPCAKE TOP

Top of the muffin to you! To separate a cupcake top from its bottom, form a "claw" with one hand over the cupcake top, holding its rim. Use that hand to gently twist and pull off the cupcake top while firmly holding the bottom of the cupcake with your other hand. Word to the wise: Cupcakes with inclusions like chocolate chips or marshmallow cream can be more difficult to separate cleanly.

TROPICAL CUPCAKE TRIFLE

SERVES 8

Not only is trifle an inspired dessert that artfully mixes cake, cream or curd, fruit, and sometimes liqueur, but it's incredibly practical, offering a simple way to transform leftover cake and fruit into something special. It's also a favorite childhood dessert of my husband, Charles. His aunt Fanny would make it for him on every special occasion, and her version was composed of ladyfingers, vanilla custard, and berries. My interpretation offers a whole new tropical take on the dessert Charles loved as a child: luscious kiwi, pineapple, and mango get a little tipsy with a splash of rum between layers of my coconut cupcakes and a cloud of vanilla-scented cream. Fanny always served her trifle in a trifle dish—a cylindrical bowl on a pedestal—but any pretty glass bowl works well. I offer a tropical flavor profile here, but consider this recipe a template you can use to create an infinite number of trifle combinations using your favorite cake, fruit, and liqueur.

2½ cups heavy cream

5 tablespoons confectioners' sugar

3½ tablespoons dark rum (optional)

1 teaspoon pure vanilla extract

1½ cups diced ripe mango

1½ cups diced ripe pineapple

1 cup diced ripe kiwi

3 tablespoons finely shredded fresh mint

1 teaspoon finely grated lime zest

12 Vanilla or Coconut Cupcake bottoms (pages 34 and 22), quartered

½ cup Dang toasted coconut chips

In the bowl of a stand mixer fitted with the whisk attachment, whip the cream, confectioners' sugar, 1 tablespoon of the rum (if using), and the vanilla until soft peaks form, 2 minutes.

In a separate bowl, fold together the mango, pineapple, kiwi, remaining 2½ tablespoons rum (if using), 2 tablespoons of the mint, and the lime zest.

Layer the ingredients in either a flat-bottomed parfait or glass bowl, using about half of the cake, cream, and fruit for each layer.

Cover and chill for at least 4 hours and up to 24 hours. Remove from the refrigerator and top with the coconut chips and remaining 1 tablespoon mint before serving.

CUPCAKE TOP WHOOPIE PIE

MAKES 1 WHOOPIE PIE

A traditional whoopie pie sandwiches a fluffy frosting between two soft cookies. Though there's nothing wrong with that, my update on the classic replaces cookies with cupcake tops bookending a pillowy cloud of homemade marshmallow cream. Feel free to mix and match the cake flavors—even using different flavored cakes for the top and bottom—to create a personalized masterpiece.

2 cupcake tops of your choice

2 to 3 tablespoons Marshmallow Frosting (page 49)

Place the cupcake tops, flat-side up, on a plate and spread the frosting onto one cupcake top. Close the sandwich and press to spread the frosting to the edges. Serve immediately.

CUPCAKE TRUFFLES

MAKES 16 TRUFFLES

One of the reasons our customers love our mini cupcakes? In addition to being adorable, they're a one- or two-bite treat. I wanted to develop another bite-sized bonbon, and these super fun cupcake truffles met every requirement. Moist cupcake crumbs and rich cream cheese frosting cling to each other like old friends, rolling easily into velvety truffles that are almost too easy to eat.

8 Dark Chocolate Cupcake bottoms (page 31) or other cupcake of your choice, broken into large pieces

⅔ cup Cream Cheese Frosting (page 14) or frosting of your choice

¼ cup unsweetened cocoa powder, sifted, for rolling (optional)

In the bowl of a stand mixer fitted with the paddle attachment, beat the cupcake bottoms and cream cheese frosting on low speed until just combined, 1 minute. Scooping 1 heaping tablespoon at a time, use your hands to roll the mixture into 1-inch balls. Set the truffles on a baking sheet and freeze until firm, 30 minutes to 1 hour. If desired, place the cocoa in a shallow bowl or a rimmed baking sheet and roll the truffles in the cocoa to coat.

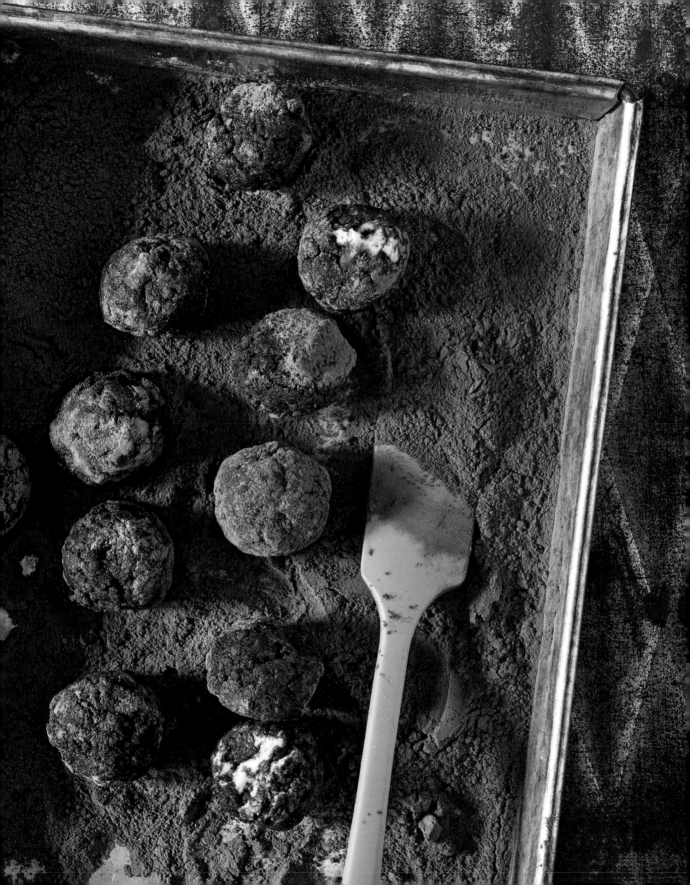

PECAN PIE CUPCAKE MILK SHAKE

MAKES 1 MILK SHAKE

At Sprinkles, we know that everything tastes better with cupcakes—and that goes for milk shakes, too! When I was brainstorming ideas for my new ice cream store, I wondered what would happen if I dropped a whole cupcake into my already-delicious milk shake. Too much? Well, I didn't think so . . . Taste it, and I think you'll agree.

1 pint (2 cups) premium butter pecan ice cream (such as Sprinkles brand!)

⅓ cup whole milk, plus more as needed

¼ cup Salted Butterscotch Sauce (page 98), plus more for drizzling

1 Cinnamon Sugar Cupcake (page 44), liner removed, broken into large pieces

Sweet Whipped Cream (page 68)

In a blender, combine the ice cream, milk, and butterscotch sauce and blend until smooth, adding extra milk 1 tablespoon at a time to achieve the desired consistency. Add the cupcake to the blender, mixing it in by hand with a long metal spoon but not turning on the blender, until the cupcake breaks into small pieces that would fit through a straw. Transfer to a tall glass, top with whipped cream, and drizzle with additional butterscotch sauce.

CHAPTER 6
COOKIES

My love for baking cookies takes me back to some of my earliest kitchen memories. Like most kids, my recollections involved a lot of dipping into the chocolate chip cookie dough before baking, but I actually looked forward to the baking process, too. Watching those balls of dough puff up, spread, and transform into delicious cookie forms was magic to me, and still is—so much so that I insisted the Sprinkles Ice Cream shops, and now cupcake bakeries, sell cookies, too! In our shops, I get to explore every cookie flavor dream I've ever had—and make many of them a reality.

The recipes in this chapter are a combination of Sprinkles cookies and new classics I either came up with myself or was lucky enough to be given by some of my cookie-loving friends.

BROWN BUTTER SNICKERDOODLES

MAKES 16 COOKIES

Just saying the word *snickerdoodle* makes me smile, and eating this cookie evokes the same reaction. Although many might think a snickerdoodle is simply a sugar cookie dressed up with cinnamon and sugar, it's actually another thing entirely. A crinkly top, a mix of crisp and crunchy textures, and a subtle tang from the addition of cream of tartar are all hallmarks of the real deal. At Sprinkles, we up the ante on this classic by using browned butter; its sophisticated, nutty flavor takes these already-scrumptious cookies to the next level. Just don't step away from that pan for a second while the butter is browning—it can go from rich and caramel-y to burnt in a matter of seconds.

1 (8-ounce) block French-style unsalted butter, such as Plugrá, plus more for greasing

3 cups all-purpose flour

2 teaspoons cream of tartar

1 teaspoon baking soda

½ teaspoon fine sea salt

2 cups plus 2 tablespoons sugar

2 large eggs

1½ tablespoons pure vanilla extract

2 teaspoons ground cinnamon

Preheat the oven to 350°F. Lightly butter 2 rimmed baking sheets.

In a medium saucepan, melt the butter over medium heat until it begins to foam, 3 to 4 minutes. Swirl the butter around in the pan until it begins to brown lightly, smell nutty, and form tiny brown flecks, 3 to 4 minutes. Remove from the heat and cool.

In a medium bowl, combine the flour, cream of tartar, baking soda, and salt.

In the bowl of a stand mixer fitted with the paddle attachment, beat the browned butter and 2 cups of the sugar on medium speed until light and fluffy, 2 to 3 minutes. Reduce the speed to low and beat in the eggs, one at a time, and the vanilla until just blended. Slowly add in the flour mixture and beat until just combined.

In a small, shallow bowl, combine the remaining 2 tablespoons sugar and the cinnamon.

Portion out 3 tablespoons of the dough at a time and form the dough into balls. Roll each ball in the cinnamon-sugar mixture and arrange the cookies on the baking sheets, five per sheet, spacing them at least 5 inches apart. Bake, rotating the sheets halfway through for even baking, until the edges are lightly browned and the centers of the cookies are set but still soft, 14 to 15 minutes for chewier cookies and 16 to 17 minutes for crispier cookies. Cool on the baking sheets for 5 minutes, then use a wide metal spatula to transfer the cookies to a wire rack to cool completely. Repeat with remaining dough.

SPRINKLES EMPLOYEES

Sprinkles started as a mom-and-pop shop, and even though we've grown, I like to think we still function with the same family feel. Many of our employees have been with us since year one or two, and our original cupcake frosters still work at the Beverly Hills Sprinkles to this day! Their tireless dedication is truly inspiring.

Our employees have gone to extreme lengths to provide legendary service for our customers. They've worked around the clock during the holiday season, packing hundreds of thousands of cupcakes. They've driven cross-country to sell cupcakes out of our Sprinklesmobile, jumped on a plane at a moment's notice to hand-deliver cupcakes to VIPs, and bought up every generator in town to keep our ovens cranking during power outages. One employee slept behind the Cupcake ATM for weeks after launch in case anything went awry. Most important, they treat our customers as they would guests at their home by forming a personal connection, leaving a lasting impression during the customer's visit, and sincerely thanking them for visiting on their way out. It's our way of ensuring that their experience in our stores is on par with the quality of our cupcakes.

Thank you, team!

THIN & CRISPY CHOCOLATE CHIP COOKIE "MONSTERS"

MAKES 14 COOKIES

When it comes to chocolate chip cookies, you're either a "chewy" or a "crispy." Personally, I've always been Team Chewy, but you've got to have great recipes for both in your baking arsenal. This giant, shatteringly crisp cookie is the product of many (admittedly delicious) trial-and-error batches. Once you mix up the ingredients, your instinct—after licking the bowl—will be to form the cookies and bake them immediately. But patience is rewarded here: letting the dough rest overnight in the fridge develops deep flavor, resulting in a cookie that has all the comforting aspects of a classic version with the benefit of added complexity. Make sure to leave ample room between the cookies on the baking sheet; while baking, they spread and bubble with a life of their own, which is why I've jokingly nicknamed them "monsters."

2¼ cups all-purpose flour

½ teaspoon baking soda

1 teaspoon fine sea salt

1 cup (2 sticks) unsalted butter, slightly softened

2½ cups sugar

½ cup lightly packed light brown sugar

1 teaspoon pure vanilla extract

1 large egg

2 cups milk chocolate or semi-sweet chocolate chips

½ teaspoon flaky sea salt, such as Maldon

In a medium bowl, whisk together the flour, baking soda, and fine sea salt.

In the bowl of a stand mixer fitted with the paddle attachment, beat the butter and sugars on medium-high speed until fluffy and smooth, 2 to 3 minutes. Turn off the mixer and scrape down the sides of the bowl with a spatula. With the mixer on low speed, add the vanilla and egg and beat until well combined. Gradually add the flour mixture and beat until just incorporated, turning the speed up to medium-high or high for a short time, if necessary, to bring the mixture together.

Using a silicone spatula, fold in the chocolate chips and the flaky sea salt. Wrap the dough in plastic wrap and refrigerate for at least a few hours and ideally overnight.

Preheat the oven to 350°F. Line two baking sheets with parchment paper.

Using a measuring cup (or a #16 disher), scoop the dough ¼ cup at a time and roll into round balls. Arrange four cookies on each prepared baking sheet, spacing them well apart; gently press down into 1-inch-thick discs. Bake until the cookies are very craggy and full of air bubbles and the edges darken, 13 to 14 minutes. Cool on the baking sheets for 5 minutes (the cookies will crisp as they cool), then use a wide metal spatula to transfer the cookies to a wire rack to cool completely. Repeat with remaining dough.

FLORIAN'S RASPBERRY MACARONS

MAKES 36 MACARONS

After shooting and co-judging over one hundred episodes of *Cupcake Wars* with renowned French pastry chef Florian Bellanger, we still may not agree on the value of red velvet cupcakes, but it hasn't prevented us from becoming the best of friends. Though he was known to be a bit stern on the show (I will never forget his catchphrase, delivered in that thick French accent: "This is just a stupid chocolate cupcake"), he has an amazing sense of humor and is, at the end of the day, a big teddy bear.

Quite frankly, with his impressive background (he was formerly the executive pastry chef for legendary bakery Fauchon and also worked under the famed pastry chef Pierre Hermé), it's only fitting that he should take his desserts very seriously. Now, Florian and his partner, Ludovic Augendre, sell their incredible MadMac confections to bakeries and hotels around the world—and have shared their luscious raspberry-flavored recipe with us. Though macarons can be intimidating, Florian made sure this recipe was not. Using raspberry preserves instead of ganache in the center saves a step, making it even more doable—even for beginners.

---

1 cup extra-fine almond flour*

¾ cup confectioners' sugar

2 large egg whites

Pinch of fine sea salt

⅓ cup sugar

Scant ½ teaspoon red gel-paste food coloring (see page 17)

1½ cups good-quality raspberry preserves with seeds, such as Bonne Maman.

In a medium bowl, sift together the almond flour and confectioners' sugar.

In the bowl of a stand mixer fitted with the whisk attachment, whip the egg whites and salt on medium speed until soft peaks form, 2 minutes. Very slowly add the sugar to the egg whites, stopping after one-third of the sugar has been added to whip for 15 seconds, then continue to slowly add the remaining sugar, stopping between each addition. After all the sugar has been added, whip for 30 seconds more until stiff peaks form. Reduce the speed to low and add the food coloring until the color is a nice, bright pink (the color will fade a bit during baking).

Working quickly, use a spatula to fold in the sifted dry ingredients by hand until just combined, folding from the center to the sides of the bowl (15 folds total), until the mixture is shiny and loose.

Preheat the oven to 350°F. Line a baking sheet with parchment paper.

Fit a piping bag with a ½-inch open tip (or snip a ½-inch opening off the end of a large zip-top bag), fill the bag with the meringue, and pipe the mixture into thirty-six 1½-inch rounds onto the prepared baking sheet. Tap the bottom of the baking sheet against the counter to flatten the rounds and release any air bubbles from the meringue. Allow the unbaked macaron shells to rest at room temperature until the tops dry slightly and don't stick to your fingertips, 15 minutes.

Bake until dry, but not browned, 13 to 14 minutes. Turn off the oven, prop open the door with a wooden spoon, and cool completely in the oven for a few hours. Remove the macaron shells from the oven, then very gently flip them and apply 1 teaspoon of the preserves to the flat side of half of the cookies. Top with the remaining cookies, flat side down, gently pressing to squeeze the filling out to the edges. Arrange the finished macarons in a single layer on a plate or a tray, cover with plastic wrap, and refrigerate overnight (this makes the macarons even more tender).

✳ Almond flour can be purchased at health food stores (make sure to buy almond flour, not almond meal, which is ground from unblanched almonds and therefore not as fine).

SPICY GINGERSNAP COOKIES

MAKES 20 COOKIES

When I set about developing the perfect ginger cookie, I had a few goals in mind: real spiciness, pronounced snap, and an irresistibility that would make it hard to keep the cookie jar full. The spice in this cookie comes in the form of dry ground and fresh grated ginger—you add the fresh toward the end to preserve its potency—and the surprise of black pepper. A roll in turbinado sugar adds extra crunch.

¾ cup all-purpose flour

½ cup whole wheat flour

1 teaspoon baking soda

1 tablespoon ground ginger

½ teaspoon ground cinnamon

¼ teaspoon finely ground black pepper

Pinch of cayenne pepper

¼ teaspoon fine sea salt

½ cup (1 stick) unsalted butter, slightly softened

½ cup lightly packed dark brown sugar

1 large egg yolk

2 tablespoons molasses, preferably robust

1 tablespoon finely grated fresh ginger

¼ cup turbinado sugar, such as Sugar In The Raw

In a large bowl, whisk together the flours, baking soda, ground ginger, cinnamon, black pepper, cayenne, and salt.

In the bowl of a stand mixer fitted with the paddle attachment, beat the butter and brown sugar on medium-high speed until fluffy, 1 to 2 minutes. Add the egg yolk and beat until incorporated, 1 minute. Add the molasses and grated ginger and beat until just combined. Reduce the speed to medium, slowly add the flour mixture, and beat until just incorporated. Cover the bowl with plastic wrap and refrigerate until firm, 1 hour.

Preheat the oven to 300°F. Line two baking sheets with parchment paper.

Place the turbinado sugar in a shallow baking dish. Using a spoon, portion out 1 tablespoon of the dough at a time and roll into round balls. Roll the balls in the turbinado sugar to coat, pressing gently to adhere the sugar to the balls. Place on the prepared baking sheets 2 inches apart and bake until browned around the edges but still slightly soft in the center, 24 to 25 minutes. Cool on the baking sheets for 5 minutes, then use a wide metal spatula to transfer the cookies to a wire rack to cool completely. The cookies will harden as they cool.

QUADRUPLE CHOCOLATE COOKIES

MAKES 20 COOKIES

When it comes to flavor, I'm all about balance. But when it comes to chocolate, more is more. So I put four different kinds of chocolate in these intensely rich cookies. The depth of flavor you get by combining bittersweet chocolate and cocoa is hard to beat, but the real surprise comes in the form of cacao nibs. Those crunchy bits deliver a huge chocolate hit. Baking these cookies for the proper amount of time yields the perfect texture: crispy on the outside, chewy within, and delicious all around.

9 ounces bittersweet chocolate, chopped

⅓ cup all-purpose flour

3 tablespoons unsweetened cocoa powder

¼ teaspoon baking powder

¼ teaspoon fine sea salt

6 tablespoons (¾ stick) unsalted butter, softened

¾ cup sugar

¼ cup lightly packed light brown sugar

¼ cup lightly packed dark brown sugar

2 teaspoons pure vanilla extract

2 large eggs

1¾ cups semisweet chocolate chunks

3 tablespoons cacao nibs

Preheat the oven to 350°F. Line two rimmed baking sheets with parchment paper.

In a microwave-safe bowl, microwave the chocolate on high for 2 to 3 minutes, stopping and stirring every 45 seconds until melted.

In a medium bowl, sift together the flour, cocoa powder, baking powder, and salt.

In the bowl of a stand mixer fitted with the paddle attachment, beat the butter and all three sugars on medium speed until light and fluffy, 2 to 3 minutes. Reduce the speed to low, add the vanilla, then the eggs one at a time and blend until incorporated and creamy. Slowly add the melted chocolate and stir until just combined. Using a silicone spatula or wooden spoon, fold in the flour mixture until just blended. Fold in the chocolate chunks and cacao nibs.

Scoop the dough 2 tablespoons at a time and drop onto the prepared baking sheets, spacing the cookies well apart. Bake until the tops are hardened but the cookies are still soft in the center, 11 to 12 minutes. Cool on baking sheets for 5 minutes, then use a wide metal spatula to transfer the cookies to a wire rack; cool completely. Repeat with remaining dough.

PEANUT BUTTER & GRAPE NUTS COOKIES

MAKES 36 COOKIES

There is something intensely satisfying about a peanut butter cookie, and this one delivers on all fronts: the gratification of rich, peanutty flavor, a pleasingly chewy texture thanks to brown sugar; and a welcome textural surprise courtesy of Grape Nuts cereal. It has an irresistible crunch and toasted barley flavor that blends perfectly here. Lest you fear that peanut butter and Grape Nuts sound more like health food than a treat, I've rolled these cookies in sugar. I promise no one will notice anything except how yummy they are!

½ cup (1 stick) butter, slightly softened, plus more for greasing

1½ cups all-purpose flour

½ teaspoon fine sea salt

½ teaspoon baking soda

1 cup sugar

¼ cup lightly packed light brown sugar

1 large egg

1 cup creamy supermarket–style peanut butter (such as Skippy)

1 teaspoon pure vanilla extract

1 cup Grape Nuts cereal

Preheat the oven to 375°F. Lightly butter two baking sheets. In a medium bowl, whisk the flour, salt, and baking soda.

In the bowl of a stand mixer fitted with the paddle attachment, beat the butter, ¾ cup of the sugar, and the brown sugar on high speed until fluffy, 1 to 2 minutes. Add the egg and beat until incorporated, 1 minute. Add the peanut butter and vanilla and beat until smooth and creamy, 1 minute. Reduce the speed to medium-low, add the flour mixture, and beat until blended, 1 minute. Fold in the Grape Nuts until just incorporated.

Place the remaining ¼ cup sugar in a shallow dish. Using a spoon, portion 1 tablespoon of the dough at a time and roll into round balls. Roll the balls in the sugar to coat. Place on the prepared baking sheets 2 inches apart and flatten with fork in a crosshatch pattern. Bake until the edges are just hard, 12 to 13 minutes. Cool on the baking sheets for 5 minutes, then use a wide metal spatula to transfer the cookies to a wire rack to cool completely. Repeat with remaining dough.

ICED MAPLE WALNUT COOKIES

MAKES 30 COOKIES

Every year as the holidays rolled around, my sister and I eagerly awaited the opportunity to bake sugar cookies with our mom. The three of us would spend hours rolling the dough, cutting out shapes, and decorating them in lively colors and patterns. These sweet, maple-licious cookies have become a more adult continuation of the tradition. After baking and cooling the cookies, a simple icing frosts the top in a pearly, sugary layer that children of all ages find hard to resist. Maple sugar—made by boiling maple sap beyond the maple syrup stage—lends a warm, distinctive sweetness that plain granulated sugar just can't deliver.

3 cups all-purpose flour

½ cup finely ground walnuts or walnut flour*

2 teaspoons baking powder

1 teaspoon fine sea salt

1 cup (2 sticks) unsalted butter, slightly softened

1 cup maple sugar**

½ cup sugar

1 large egg

1 tablespoon pure maple syrup

1 teaspoon pure vanilla extract

In a medium bowl, whisk together the flour, ground walnuts, baking powder, and salt.

In the bowl of a stand mixer fitted with the paddle attachment, beat the butter and both sugars on high speed until fluffy, 2 minutes. Add the egg, maple syrup, and vanilla and beat until incorporated, 1 minute. Reduce the speed to low, slowly add the flour mixture, and beat until just incorporated, 1 to 2 minutes.

Divide the dough in half, wrap each half in plastic, and chill until firm, 2 to 3 hours or up to overnight.

Preheat the oven to 375°F. Line two baking sheets with parchment paper.

On a lightly floured surface, roll out the dough to ⅓-inch thickness and cut out circles or maple leaf shapes with a cookie cutter. Gather the scraps into a ball, wrap them in plastic wrap, chill them for 15 minutes, reroll the dough, and cut out more cookies. Using an offset spatula, transfer the cookies to the prepared baking sheets, spacing them at least 2 inches apart, and bake until the edges are golden and the cookies puff slightly, 8 to 9 minutes. Cool on

MAPLE GLAZE

4 cups confectioners' sugar, sifted

7 tablespoons whole milk

¾ teaspoon maple extract or maple syrup

In a bowl, whisk the confectioners' sugar, milk, and maple extract until smooth. One at a time, dip the entire top of the cooled cookies into the glaze, tilting to drip off excess, and place the glazed cookies on the racks. Allow the glaze to harden.

the baking sheets for 5 minutes, then use a wide metal spatula to transfer the cookies to a wire rack to cool completely.

Arrange each rack with the cooled cookies on top of a cooled baking sheet.

* To make your own walnut flour, process raw walnuts in a food processor until fine (but make sure not to overprocess, which will create walnut butter!).

** Maple sugar can be found in natural foods stores, many supermarkets, and online. Well-known brands include Coombs Family Farms and Shady Maple.

JANET'S BROWNIE BRITTLE

MAKES 30 PIECES

My life was forever changed when I enrolled in pastry school in San Francisco after the Internet start-up bust of the early 2000s. Janet Dalton, former executive pastry chef at the venerable Postrio restaurant and *San Francisco* magazine's 2004 "pastry chef of the year," had taken some time off from the restaurant world to teach. To say that Janet was a great teacher is an understatement. She was inspiring, funny, and completely fearless. There was no pastry problem she couldn't solve and no kitchen she couldn't lead, but beyond that, this woman fly-fished, climbed mountains, and traveled to the outer edges of the world. I always kept in touch with Janet…and she was always up to something incredible: consulting on amazing new restaurants, developing candy for Williams-Sonoma…the list goes on.

So when Charles and I decided to expand the Sprinkles brand with an ice cream concept, Janet was the first person we called. She helped us immeasurably with her vast ice cream knowledge. This is one of Janet's latest recipe discoveries, and I'm already hooked. It can be crumbled into small bits to be used as a topping, but I prefer it broken into large, freeform shards and eaten as a snack or cookie. My kids agree!

Cooking spray

2 ounces bittersweet chocolate

6 tablespoons unsalted butter

1 cup sugar

½ teaspoon instant espresso powder

1 teaspoon pure vanilla extract

½ cup all-purpose flour

2 tablespoons unsweetened cocoa powder

¼ teaspoon baking soda

¼ teaspoon fine sea salt

2 large egg whites

½ cup (2½ ounces) finely chopped semisweet chocolate

Preheat the oven to 325°F. Line a baking sheet with parchment paper and lightly coat the parchment with cooking spray.

In a microwave-safe bowl, microwave the bittersweet chocolate and butter on high for 2 to 3 minutes, stopping and stirring every 45 seconds until melted. Stir in the sugar, espresso powder, and vanilla. In a separate bowl, whisk together the flour, cocoa powder, baking soda, and salt.

In the bowl of a stand mixer fitted with the whisk attachment, whip the egg whites on medium-high speed until frothy, 3 to 4

minutes (they should resemble well-lathered shampoo). Add the chocolate mixture and whip until just combined. Reduce the speed to low, add the flour mixture, and whip until just combined.

Using an offset spatula, spread the batter over the prepared baking sheet into as thin a layer as possible. Sprinkle the semisweet chocolate on top and bake until crisp and the top is slightly cracked, 24 to 25 minutes.* Cool the brittle completely on the baking sheet. Using your hands, break up the brittle.

* If you want the brittle to have uniformly sized pieces, remove the pan from the oven after 20 minutes and use a knife to score the brittle into pieces of your preferred size. Return the pan to the oven and bake for 5 minutes, cool in the pan, and break along the score marks.

MOCHA CHIP MERINGUES

MAKES 24 MERINGUES

My mother first taught me how to make meringues as a kid when my family was living in Indonesia. If you've ever worked with this fluffy stuff before, you know that humidity and meringue don't mix—something I quickly learned while living on the equator. I like to think that my training in the most grueling of environments made me a better meringue maker, and it definitely gave me a profound respect for the delicacy of whipped egg whites that I possess to this day.

I take my time and follow the rules fastidiously: cracking the eggs when cold, whisking them when they come to room temperature, making sure my mixing bowl is free of any oil that might prevent the eggs from forming a billowy cloud.

Back in the day, I used a handheld whisk and worked up quite a sweat, but now I prefer a stand mixer fitted with the whisk attachment, which incorporates air more quickly and yields a more stable meringue. These meringues have that ideal crisp exterior and slightly chewy interior, and the espresso adds a nice coffee kick along with a beautiful café au lait color.

3 large egg whites, at room temperature

1 teaspoon distilled white vinegar

1 cup granulated or superfine sugar

1½ teaspoons pure vanilla extract

1 tablespoon instant espresso powder, such as Medaglia d'Oro brand

½ cup mini chocolate chips

Pinch of fine sea salt

Arrange a rack in the center of the oven and preheat the oven to 350°F. Line two baking sheets with parchment paper.

In the bowl of a stand mixer fitted with the whisk attachment, whip the egg whites and vinegar until foamy, 1 minute. Add half the sugar 1 tablespoon at a time, then add the vanilla. Add the remaining sugar ¼ cup at a time, then the espresso powder, and beat until the sugar has dissolved and stiff peaks form, 5 minutes total. Using a silicone spatula, gently fold in the chocolate chips and the salt until just incorporated.

Using a spoon, portion 1 heaping tablespoon of meringue at a time onto the prepared baking sheets, spacing them at least 3 inches apart. Place in the oven and turn off the oven. Leave the cookies in the oven for 5 hours; they will develop a crisp shell and tender, slightly chewy interior.

CRUNCHY COFFEE TOFFEE SHORTBREAD

MAKES 16 SQUARES

Sometimes, it's the recipes you think will be the easiest that become the greatest challenges. Such was the case with this shortbread. I tasted batch after batch until one finally met my requirements: sandy, buttery, crunchy, and perfectly sweet. I included a few add-ins that made it feel extra-special: cacao nibs, ground coffee, and little bits of toffee that bake right into the surface.

1¼ cups all-purpose flour

2 tablespoons cornstarch

1½ teaspoons ground coffee beans

½ teaspoon fine sea salt

¾ cup (1½ sticks) unsalted butter, slightly softened

⅓ cup sugar

3 tablespoons cacao nibs

¼ cup crushed hard toffee bits (such as Heath Bits 'O Brickle)

6 ounces semisweet chocolate, finely chopped

Preheat the oven to 325°F. Line an 8-inch square baking pan with two strips of parchment paper that fit the pan both vertically and horizontally, leaving a 2-inch overhang on all sides.

In a small bowl, whisk together the flour, cornstarch, coffee, and salt. In the bowl of a stand mixer fitted with the paddle attachment, beat the butter and sugar on medium-high speed until creamy, 2 to 3 minutes. Reduce the speed to medium-low, add the flour mixture, and beat until just incorporated (the dough will be pretty stiff). Beat in the cacao nibs until just incorporated. Press the dough into the prepared pan and prick the surface all over with a fork.

Bake for 20 minutes, then sprinkle the toffee bits on top and bake until the edges are golden brown, 14 to 15 minutes more. Cool slightly in the pan, then cut into squares or rectangles, leaving them in the pan, and cool completely.

Line a baking sheet with parchment paper. In a microwave-safe bowl, microwave the chocolate, stopping and stirring every 45 seconds until melted, 2 to 3 minutes total. Working one at a time, dip the cookies halfway into the chocolate, allowing the excess to drip into the bowl. Set the dipped cookies on the prepared baking sheet as you work. Allow the chocolate to cool and set (to speed up the process, refrigerate the dipped cookies for 15 minutes).

CHEWY CHOCOLATE CHIP COOKIES

MAKES 14 TO 16 COOKIES

I have been spellbound by chocolate chip cookies since I was a little girl. How such a simple treat could be so complex, with so many variations all made from the same basic ingredients, mystifies me to this day. For me, the perfect chewy version consists of a crisp exterior that gives way to a gooey interior studded with still-melty chocolate chips, and that is exactly the style of cookie I created for Sprinkles. Melting the butter before mixing it in, then resting the dough, allows flavor and texture to mature and develops complexity. Although it requires more patience, I promise the extra wait is worth it.

2¼ cups all-purpose flour

1 teaspoon baking soda

1 teaspoon fine sea salt

1 cup (2 sticks) unsalted butter, melted and still warm

1¼ cups sugar

¼ cup lightly packed light brown sugar

1 teaspoon pure vanilla extract

1 large egg

2 large egg yolks

2 cups semisweet chocolate chips

In a medium bowl, whisk together the flour, baking soda, and salt.

In the bowl of a stand mixer fitted with the paddle attachment, beat the butter and sugars on medium speed until fluffy and smooth, 2 to 3 minutes. Turn off the mixer and scrape down the sides of the bowl with a silicone spatula. With the mixer on low speed, add the vanilla, egg, and egg yolks and beat until incorporated. Gradually add the flour mixture and beat until just incorporated, turning the speed up to medium-high or high for a few seconds if necessary to bring the mixture together. Using a silicone spatula, fold in the chocolate chips by hand. Wrap the dough in plastic wrap and refrigerate for at least a few hours, but ideally overnight.

Preheat the oven to 350°F. Line two baking sheets with parchment paper. Scoop the dough ¼ cup at a time and roll into round balls. Arrange four cookies on each prepared baking sheet, spacing them well apart; do not press down. Bake until the tops are golden brown, 11 to 12 minutes. Cool on the baking sheets for 5 minutes, then use a wide metal spatula to transfer the cookies to a wire rack to cool completely. Repeat with remaining dough.

CHAPTER 7

BROWNIES & BARS

One of the issues I encountered when I began baking cupcakes was how to transport them. We take it for granted now, but before the "cupcake rush," there were no containers or boxes specifically designed for the task. Hard to imagine, but true! Thankfully, brownies and bars have never had that problem. Baked in a square pan—made from either trusty metal or pretty ceramic—they're ready to go anywhere in a pinch. I always like to line my baking pans with overlapping pieces of parchment, using the overhanging ends to form "handles" that make pulling the bars straight out of the pan—and getting a nice clean cut—a snap. That way your bars are display ready, whether you serve them stacked or side by side.

SMOKED ALMOND CHOCOLATE COCONUT BARS

MAKES 20 BARS

This recipe proves that you don't need a million ingredients to create something new and exciting. The crunchy, buttery base is a snap, and the contrast of tastes and textures in the crisp and creamy, sweet and smoky topping is a welcome surprise. Though I don't typically recommend using chocolate chips for melting, I've found that they work well in this instance if that's all you have in your cupboard.

FOR THE BASE:

¾ cup (1½ sticks) unsalted butter, softened, plus more for greasing

1½ cups all-purpose flour

¼ teaspoon baking powder

¼ teaspoon salt

⅔ cup sugar

FOR THE TOPPING:

12 ounces milk chocolate, chopped (or 2 cups milk chocolate chips)

1½ cups smoked, roasted, and salted almonds, chopped

⅔ cup unsweetened coconut flakes, lightly toasted

MAKE THE BASE:

Preheat the oven to 350°F. Generously butter the bottom and sides of a 9-inch square pan and line with two strips of parchment paper that fit the pan both vertically and horizontally, leaving a 2-inch overhang on all sides, and generously butter the parchment.

In a medium bowl, whisk together the flour, baking powder, and salt.

In the bowl of a stand mixer fitted with the paddle attachment, beat the butter and sugar until creamy, 2 minutes. Add the flour mixture and beat until incorporated, 1 minute.

Press the dough into the prepared pan and bake until golden, 19 to 20 minutes. Transfer pan to a wire rack and cool completely.

MAKE THE TOPPING:

In a microwave-safe bowl, microwave the chocolate on high for 2 to 3 minutes, stopping and stirring every 45 seconds until melted. Stir ¾ cup of the almonds and ⅓ cup of the coconut into the chocolate, then spread the chocolate over the cooled base in the pan. Sprinkle with the remaining ¾ cup almonds and ⅓ cup coconut, pressing gently to help adhere them to the chocolate. Refrigerate for 30 minutes to harden, then cut into 20 equal-size bars.

DATE-HONEY SESAME BARS

MAKES 32 BARS

Middle Eastern ingredients are perfectly suited to desserts, where they bridge the gap between the exotic and the familiar. Not only are honey and dates both natural sweeteners, but each has its own unique flavor profile, which we put to great use in these bars. A lightly spiced, sesame-studded oat crust sandwiches the sweet filling, resulting in an indulgent but not overly rich dessert, perfectly suited for any occasion.

FOR THE FILLING:

2 cups chopped pitted dates

1 cup cold water

¼ cup lightly packed light brown sugar

¼ cup honey

¼ cup raw slivered almonds, finely ground

1½ teaspoons pure vanilla extract

1 teaspoon finely grated orange zest

FOR THE CRUST:

¾ cup (1½ sticks) unsalted butter, slightly softened, plus more for greasing

1½ cups all-purpose flour

1½ cups quick-cooking oats

½ teaspoon ground cinnamon

⅛ teaspoon freshly grated nutmeg

¼ teaspoon finely grated orange zest

½ teaspoon baking soda

½ teaspoon fine sea salt

1 cup lightly packed light brown sugar

2 tablespoons raw sesame seeds

MAKE THE FILLING:

In a food processor, pulse the dates until finely diced, 30 to 40 pulses. Transfer the dates to a medium saucepan and add the water, brown sugar, and honey. Bring to a boil, reduce the heat to medium-low, and cook, stirring occasionally, until the mixture thickens and resembles a thick jam, 10 to 11 minutes. Remove from the heat and stir in the almonds, vanilla, and orange zest. Transfer to a bowl and cool while you make the crust.

MAKE THE CRUST:

Preheat the oven to 375°F. Lightly butter a 9 x 13-inch baking pan. Line the pan with two strips of parchment paper that fit both

vertically and horizontally, leaving a 2-inch overhang on all sides, and generously butter the parchment.

In a medium bowl, combine the flour, oats, cinnamon, nutmeg, orange zest, baking soda, and salt.

In the bowl of a stand mixer fitted with the paddle attachment, beat the butter and brown sugar on medium-high speed until light and fluffy, 2 to 3 minutes. Reduce the speed to low and slowly add the flour mixture until just combined; the mixture will be crumbly, but should stick together when pressed between your thumb and index finger.

Sprinkle half the dough evenly into the baking pan. Using your fingers, lightly press the dough into an even layer. Using an offset spatula, spread the date mixture over the crust, then sprinkle the remaining dough over the filling and press to create an even top crust. Sprinkle with sesame seeds and bake until browned and set, 25 minutes. While still warm, cut into 32 equal-size squares. Transfer the pan to a wire rack and cool completely.

LEMON-LIME ICEBOX BARS

MAKES 16 BARS

Named for the time they spend chilling out in the fridge, icebox bars are a great foil for a variety of flavors—the common denominator being extra-cool creaminess in every bite. I start out with a short crust that stays flaky to the end, and since I'm a sucker for citrus, I add a quadruple dose thanks to the zest *and* juice of both lemons and limes. That tartness balances out a rich, silky filling made with a combination of cream cheese and condensed milk—with just a touch of gelatin to help it hold together.

FOR THE CRUST:

½ cup (1 stick) cold unsalted butter, cut into pieces, plus more for greasing

1 cup all-purpose flour

¼ cup sugar

⅛ teaspoon fine sea salt

½ teaspoon finely grated lemon zest

½ teaspoon finely grated lime zest

FOR THE FILLING:

6 ounces (¾ cup) cream cheese, slightly softened

¼ cup sugar

⅛ teaspoon fine sea salt

1 teaspoon finely grated lemon zest

¼ cup fresh lemon juice

1 teaspoon finely grated lime zest

¼ cup fresh lime juice

1 teaspoon pure vanilla extract

1½ teaspoons powdered gelatin

2 tablespoons cold water

2 tablespoons warm water

1 (14-ounce) can sweetened condensed milk

MAKE THE CRUST:

Preheat the oven to 350°F. Butter a 9-inch square baking pan, line the pan with two strips of parchment paper that fit the pan both vertically and horizontally, leaving a 2-inch overhang on all sides, and generously butter the parchment.

In a food processor, pulse the flour, sugar, salt, and lemon and lime zests until incorporated. Add the butter and pulse until the dough starts to come together but is still somewhat crumbly, 25 pulses. Using your fingers, evenly press the dough into the bottom of the prepared baking pan, then prick holes all over the dough with a fork or a wooden skewer. Bake until the crust is golden brown, 13 to 14 minutes. Transfer the pan to a wire rack and cool completely.

MAKE THE FILLING:

In the bowl of a stand mixer fitted with the whisk attachment, whip the cream cheese, sugar, and salt on medium-high speed until fluffy, 1 to 2 minutes. Reduce the speed to low, add the lemon zest and juice, lime zest and juice, and the vanilla, and whip until combined, 1 minute.

Sprinkle the gelatin across the bottom of a small bowl, sprinkle with the cold water, and allow the gelatin to bloom for 5 minutes. Add the warm water and stir to dissolve the gelatin, making sure it's totally dissolved. Add the gelatin and condensed milk to the cream cheese mixture and whip until soft peaks form, 1 to 2 minutes.

Spread the filling over the crust, cover the pan with plastic wrap, and chill until set, at least 6 hours or up to overnight. Uncover and lift the bars out of the pan using the parchment. Cut into 16 equal-size bars.

FUDGY BROWNIES

MAKES 16 BROWNIES

I was quite young when I made my first brownie recipe, which I chose for its deceptively simple list of ingredients. With only five main elements—flour, butter, sugar, eggs, and chocolate—I was able to whip up a batch of these on a whim with items my mother kept stocked in our pantry. I quickly came to learn that while the method may have been easy, I could perfect the texture—especially that chocolate quotient—by adjusting the recipe's proportions. Like a mad scientist, I'd tweak each component ever so slightly, batch after batch, until I achieved the desired result: my classic brownies, distinguished by their fudgy interiors and shiny, crackly top—my take on a uniquely American creation that never goes out of style.

6 tablespoons European-style butter, such as Plugrá, plus more for greasing

1 cup sugar

¼ teaspoon fine sea salt

6 ounces bittersweet chocolate, chopped

2 large eggs

¼ cup all-purpose flour

1 teaspoon pure vanilla extract

Preheat the oven to 350°F. Generously butter the bottom and sides of an 8-inch square pan and line the pan with two strips of parchment paper that fit the pan both vertically and horizontally, leaving a 2-inch overhang on all sides.

In a small bowl, combine the sugar and salt.

In a medium microwave-safe bowl, microwave the butter and chocolate on high for 2 to 3 minutes, stopping every 45 seconds to stir until melted and smooth. Stir in the sugar mixture until blended. Whisk in the eggs one at a time until fully incorporated, then whisk in the flour and vanilla until the mixture is smooth and glossy. Pour the batter into the prepared pan and bake until the top is set and slightly shiny (the brownies should not spring back when pressed), 25 to 26 minutes. Transfer the pan to a wire rack, cool completely, and cut into 16 equal-size squares.

PEANUT BUTTER & JELLY BARS

MAKES 16 BARS

Having spent part of my childhood overseas, I know how strong the passion for a local delicacy can be. As an ex-pat (with Australian friends who really loved their Vegemite, a yeasty, salty spread that appeared on an episode of *Cupcake Wars*) I came to realize how strongly I felt about peanut butter, an all-American treat. Even more reason to love it: its creamy, nutty goodness can be the foundation for a great dessert, such as these incredibly decadent—and very American— peanut butter and jelly bars.

7 tablespoons unsalted butter, slightly softened, plus more for greasing

1¼ cups all-purpose flour

½ teaspoon baking powder

1¼ teaspoons fine sea salt

½ cup sugar

½ cup lightly packed light brown sugar

2 large eggs

1 teaspoon pure vanilla extract

¾ cup chunky supermarket-style peanut butter

1 cup good-quality blackberry or raspberry jam (seeded is fine)

¼ cup chopped salted roasted peanuts

Preheat the oven to 350°F. Generously butter an 8-inch square baking pan. Line the pan with two strips of parchment paper that fit the pan both vertically and horizontally, leaving a 2-inch overhang on all sides, and generously butter the parchment. In a medium bowl, whisk together flour, baking powder, and salt.

In the bowl of a stand mixer fitted with the paddle attachment, beat the butter and sugars on medium-high speed until light and fluffy, 2 to 3 minutes. Add the eggs and vanilla and beat until blended, 1 to 2 minutes. Add the peanut butter and beat until combined, 1 minute. Lower the speed to medium and add the flour mixture in two additions, beating until blended after each addition. Press two-thirds of the dough into the bottom of the pan, then spread the jam evenly over the top.

In a small bowl, combine the peanuts and the remaining dough with your hands, then arrange the mixture in 1-inch clusters evenly over the jam. Bake until the topping is lightly golden and the peanuts are fragrant, 30 minutes. Transfer the pan to a wire rack and cool completely. Lift the bars out of the pan using the parchment and cut into 2-inch squares.

BUTTERSCOTCH MILK CHOCOLATE BARS

MAKES 12 BARS

In trying to find a way to combine as many of my favorite things as possible into one dessert, I landed on these over-the-top, densely decadent bars. The goal here was sheer, crazy deliciousness, and even I was surprised by how incredible this recipe turned out! Once baked, layers of creamy condensed milk, butterscotch, chocolate, coconut, and walnuts sink into a graham cracker crust to form something so sweet and good you'll want to keep a supply on hand at all times. Bonus: They keep for up to a week on the counter!

---

4 tablespoons (½ stick) unsalted butter, melted, plus more for greasing

7 whole graham crackers (14 squares)

1 (14-ounce) can sweetened condensed milk

1 cup butterscotch chips

½ cup semisweet chocolate chips

½ cup sweetened, shredded coconut shavings

1½ cups whole shelled unsalted walnuts

½ teaspoon fleur de sel

Preheat the oven to 350°F. Butter an 8-inch square baking pan, line the pan with two strips of parchment paper that fit the pan both vertically and horizontally, leaving a 2-inch overhang on all sides, and generously butter the parchment.

Break up the graham crackers, then process them in a food processor until fine crumbs form, 30 seconds. Transfer the crumbs to a small bowl and stir together with the melted butter until coated (the mixture will be relatively crumbly). Press the crumbs evenly over the bottom of the prepared baking dish, then pour the condensed milk on top of the graham cracker crust, scraping all the condensed milk out of the can with a silicone spatula. Sprinkle the butterscotch and chocolate chips on top of the condensed milk, then sprinkle the coconut on top of the chips. Finally, sprinkle the walnuts evenly over the top, pressing down firmly until the mixture soaks up to the walnut layer.

Bake until the center is set, 30 minutes. While still warm, sprinkle the top with the fleur de sel. Transfer the pan to a wire rack to cool completely, then lift the bars out of the pan using the parchment and cut into 12 equal-size squares.

BLACKBERRY ICEBOX BARS

MAKES 16 BARS

This gorgeous, rosy-pink refrigerator dessert brings to mind an old adage: "Good things come to those who wait." True, making the simple berry jam is a snap. And whipping up the filling to spoon over a delicious crust, made crunchy with a bit of turbinado sugar, is also relatively quick! The real secret is to let this one chill for a good, long time. The generous amount of whipped cream needs time to settle, and you'll know it's ready when the topping has sunk down into itself, allowing the bars to be cut into clean, uniform squares. Not to worry: taking them out and cutting them a little early makes for a slightly messier—but no less delicious—experience.

FOR THE BLACKBERRY JAM:

2 cups fresh blackberries

1 cup sugar

3 tablespoons fresh lemon juice

FOR THE CRUST:

¾ cup (1½ sticks) cold unsalted butter, cut into pieces, plus more for greasing

1¼ cups all-purpose flour

¼ cup cornstarch

¼ cup sugar

1 tablespoon turbinado sugar, such as Sugar In The Raw

¼ teaspoon fine sea salt

1 teaspoon pure vanilla extract

1 large egg yolk, at room temperature

FOR THE FILLING:

1¾ cups heavy cream

1 teaspoon pure vanilla extract

2 (8-ounce) packages cream cheese, at room temperature

½ cup sugar

MAKE THE BLACKBERRY JAM:

Combine the blackberries, sugar, lemon juice, and 1 tablespoon water in a small saucepan, bring to a boil, and boil about 5 minutes, mashing the blackberries with a potato masher or fork until broken up. Reduce the heat to medium-low and simmer until thickened and small to medium bubbles begin to form on the surface of the mixture, some foam appears, and the mixture coats the back of a spoon, 22 to 23 minutes. Transfer to a bowl and refrigerate for 10 minutes, give it a stir, cover, and refrigerate until cool to the touch, 45 minutes to 1 hour.

(Continued)

MAKE THE CRUST:

Preheat the oven to 325°F. Butter a 9-inch square baking pan, line the pan with two strips of parchment paper that fit the pan both vertically and horizontally, leaving a 2-inch overhang on all sides, and generously butter the parchment.

In the bowl of a stand mixer fitted with the paddle attachment, mix the flour, cornstarch, sugars, and salt on low speed until just combined. Add the butter and beat until the butter is evenly dispersed and broken down into pea-size pieces; the mixture will still be dry and crumbly. Add the vanilla and egg yolk and beat until the dough just comes together, 15 seconds, making sure not to overmix.

Turn the dough out into the baking pan and gently press it into an even layer. Prick the dough all over with a fork or a wooden skewer and bake until just barely golden brown on the edges, 26 to 27 minutes. Transfer the pan to a wire rack and cool completely.

MAKE THE FILLING:

Remove the jam from the refrigerator and allow it to come to room temperature.

In the bowl of a stand mixer fitted with the whisk attachment, whip the cream and vanilla on medium speed until soft, billowy peaks form, 2 to 3 minutes; transfer to a bowl. In the same mixer bowl, whip the cream cheese, cooled jam, and sugar on high speed until light and airy (the mixture will have the consistency of thick frosting), 3 to 4 minutes. Using a silicone spatula, fold in the whipped cream. Fold in the jam until just combined and the mixture is uniform in color. Gently spread the mixture over the cooled crust, smooth the top with an offset spatula, cover with plastic wrap, and refrigerate until chilled, at least overnight or, even better, 12 hours. Cut into 16 equal-size squares.

COCOA MINT BROWNIES

MAKES 16 BROWNIES

I set about developing this recipe with a gold standard in mind: Andes mints, those little rectangular foil-wrapped chocolates with a smooth ingot of minty white chocolate sandwiched right in the middle. Unlike my Fudgy Brownies (page 150), these are a bit cakier, but still chocolaty enough to stand up to a rich white layer I infuse with sprigs of fresh mint. By using coconut oil—which hardens when chilled—as a main ingredient in the ganache, I achieved the signature solid, creamy layer.

FOR THE BROWNIES:

½ cup (1 stick) unsalted butter, plus more for greasing

⅓ cup all-purpose flour

⅓ cup unsweetened cocoa powder

¼ teaspoon fine sea salt

2 ounces bittersweet chocolate

¾ cup sugar

1 teaspoon pure vanilla extract

2 large eggs

FOR THE MINT GANACHE:

¼ cup refined coconut oil

2 tablespoons heavy cream

4 to 5 sprigs fresh mint

6 ounces white chocolate, chopped, or white chocolate chips

MAKE THE BROWNIES:

Preheat the oven to 350°F. Butter a 9-inch square baking pan, line the pan with two strips of parchment paper that fit the pan both vertically and horizontally, leaving a 2-inch overhang on all sides, and generously butter the parchment.

In a medium bowl, sift together the flour, cocoa powder, and salt.

In a separate microwave-safe medium bowl, microwave the butter and chocolate on high for 2 to 3 minutes, stopping and stirring every 45 seconds until melted and smooth. Cool slightly, whisk in the sugar and vanilla, then whisk in the eggs until incorporated. Gradually add the flour mixture until just combined. Pour the batter into the prepared pan and bake until the brownies begin to pull away from the edges of the pan and a toothpick inserted into the center comes out clean, 17 to 18 minutes. Transfer the pan to a wire rack and cool completely.

(Continued)

MAKE THE GANACHE:

In a small saucepan, bring the coconut oil, cream, and mint to a simmer. Remove from the heat, cover, and let steep for at least 30 minutes or up to 4 hours, or more, depending on your preferred level of mint intensity.

In a microwave-safe bowl, microwave the white chocolate on high for 2 to 3 minutes, stopping and stirring every 45 seconds until melted.

Remove the mint sprigs from the coconut oil–cream mixture, squeeze any cream back into the pot, discard the mint, and whisk the warm coconut oil–cream mixture into the melted chocolate just until smooth. Spread evenly over the brownies and chill until the ganache hardens, 30 minutes. Lift the brownies out of the pan using the parchment and cut into 16 equal-size pieces.

NUTELLA RICE KRISPIES TREATS

MAKES 16 SQUARES

The first thing I ever "baked" with each of my sons were Rice Krispies treats. They are irresistible to kids, and the process—requiring only a microwave and a bowl—is innately kid-friendly. Without fear of burning little fingers on hot pans or stovetops, you can focus all your attention on stirring that sticky marshmallow into the crisp cereal puffs as quickly as possible before patting it all into a buttered pan. Though we all still love the tried-and-true original, this grown-up version, made with chocolate and hazelnut and then finished with a scattering of toasted hazelnuts, takes the childhood treat to another level entirely.

5 tablespoons unsalted butter, plus more for greasing the pan

6 cups toasted rice cereal, such as Rice Krispies

1 (10-ounce) bag mini marshmal-lows (6 cups)

1 cup chocolate-hazelnut spread, such as Nutella

½ cup chopped hazelnuts, lightly toasted and cooled

Grease a 9-inch baking pan with butter.

Pour the cereal into a large bowl. In a medium saucepan, melt the marshmallows and butter together over low heat, whisking until smooth, 7 to 8 minutes. Add the chocolate-hazelnut spread, stir until well combined, then immediately pour the marshmallow mixture over the cereal; the mixture will cool quickly and become difficult to stir, so work quickly to combine and then immediately press the mixture into the prepared pan. Sprinkle the hazelnuts over the top, pressing lightly to help them adhere to the mixture.

Cool completely and cut into 16 equal-size squares.

CHAPTER 8

LOAVES & QUICK BREADS

There is something so encouraging about the name "quick bread," which promises that in no time at all, you will be enjoying the fruits of your simple and speedy labor. In truth, the name "quick" comes from the necessity to bake them immediately after mixing, since the leavening agent (either baking soda or baking powder) has been activated by the batter and has begun to work immediately. Regardless of the technicalities, quick breads are delicious and relatively speedy. Easy to make, easier to love!

ESPRESSO & CREAM MARBLE POUND CAKE

SERVES 10

There is nothing simpler than a traditional pound cake, which gets its name from the recipe's easy-to-memorize original proportions: one pound each of flour, butter, eggs, and sugar! It may be simple, but its sweet, buttery flavor gives it a timelessness that appeals to absolutely everybody. Here, I took the classic and reworked the recipe to make the cake as light as it is moist. I then woke it up with a jolt of espresso that gets swirled into the batter for a beautiful marbled effect. It's like a sweet, creamy cappuccino in every bite.

¾ cup (1½ sticks) unsalted butter, slightly softened, plus more for greasing

1¾ cups all-purpose flour, sifted, plus more for flouring the pan

2 tablespoons instant espresso powder, such as Medaglia d'Oro

1 teaspoon boiling water

½ teaspoon fine sea salt

1¾ cups sugar

3 large eggs, at room temperature

½ cup heavy cream

1 teaspoon pure vanilla extract

Preheat the oven to 325°F. Butter and flour an 8½ x 4½-inch loaf pan; tap out the excess flour.

In a small bowl or ramekin, dissolve the espresso in the boiling water.

In a medium bowl, whisk together the flour and salt.

In the bowl of a stand mixer fitted with the paddle attachment, beat the butter and sugar on medium-high speed until smooth, 2 to 3 minutes. Reduce the speed to low and add the eggs one at a time, blending after each addition until well incorporated. Add half the flour mixture, then the cream and vanilla, then the remaining flour mixture, beating until just blended after each addition.

Divide the batter evenly between two bowls. Fold the espresso into one of the bowls until fully incorporated and the batter is uniform in color. Spoon a scoop of the vanilla batter into the corner of the prepared loaf pan so that it takes up half the width of the pan. Spoon a scoop of the coffee batter next to it so that there is a row of two squares across the pan. For the next row, begin with a scoop of coffee batter and then vanilla batter and continue, alternating every

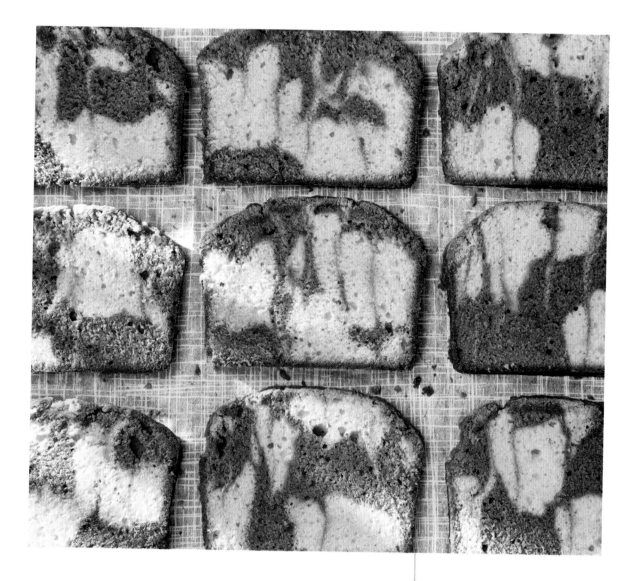

row, so that you create a checkerboard pattern with the different batters across the loaf pan. Very gently smooth the top of the batter with an offset spatula or knife, then insert a dinner knife or wooden skewer into the batter until it hits the bottom of the pan and move it in a swirling motion a few times across the pan to create a marbled effect. Gently tap the pan against the countertop to eliminate air bubbles.

Bake for 50 minutes, then cover the cake with aluminum foil and bake until a toothpick inserted into the center comes out covered in crumbs but not wet batter, 40 minutes more. Transfer to a wire rack and cool for 20 minutes, then tilt the cake out of the pan onto the rack and cool completely.

BROWN BUTTER CHOCOLATE CHIP BANANA BREAD

SERVES 12

Banana bread is one of those treats that can be pulled out for any occasion; even more important, everyone loves it. This banana bread has all the qualities you're looking for: clear banana flavor; a moist, but not dense, crumb; crunchy nuts; and—of course—chocolate chips! But it also hides a tasty secret: browned butter, which creates a deeper, more sophisticated flavor that will leave everyone asking for *your* banana bread recipe.

½ cup (1 stick) unsalted butter, plus more for greasing

¾ cup plus 2 teaspoons all-purpose flour, plus more for flouring the pan

¾ cup whole wheat pastry flour

½ cup sugar

¼ cup lightly packed light brown sugar

¾ teaspoon baking soda

½ teaspoon fine sea salt

2 large eggs

2 tablespoons full-fat sour cream

1¼ cups mashed very ripe banana (3 large bananas)

⅔ cup bittersweet chocolate chips

1 teaspoon pure vanilla extract

¾ cup chopped toasted walnuts

Preheat the oven to 350° F. Butter and flour an 8½ x 4½-inch loaf pan; tap out the excess flour. In a medium saucepan, melt the butter over medium heat until it begins to foam, 3 to 4 minutes. Swirl the butter around in the pan until it begins to brown and smell nutty, 3 to 4 minutes. Remove the saucepan from the heat.

In a large bowl, whisk together ¾ cup of the all-purpose flour, the whole wheat flour, both sugars, baking soda, and salt. In a medium bowl, whisk together the eggs and sour cream until smooth, then stir in the mashed banana and cooled brown butter. Fold the egg mixture into the flour mixture until just blended. In a small bowl, toss the chocolate chips with the vanilla, then toss with the remaining 2 teaspoons flour. Fold the coated chips and the walnuts into the batter. Pour the batter into the prepared pan and bake, rotating midway through for even baking, until a toothpick inserted into the center comes out clean and the cake springs back when gently pressed, 55 to 60 minutes. Transfer to a wire rack and cool for 20 minutes, then tilt the bread onto the rack and cool completely.

JULIA ROBERTS'S BANANA HEMP HEART MUFFINS

MAKES 12 MUFFINS

The day I was fortunate enough to meet Julia Roberts, I was instantly struck by her effortless beauty. I have long admired her healthy, natural, California lifestyle, and these banana muffins exemplify everything that inspires me about Julia. I mean, how can you *not* love that one of the most famous women in the world takes the time to bake these healthful muffins for her children? Unbelievably delicious and moist, these are the perfect way to start your morning. They're pumped up with omega-rich hemp hearts and flaxseed meal and, for good measure, antioxidant-rich, crunchy chia seeds. Coconut sugar lends an extra note of sweetness that complements the slight toastiness you'll love in these muffins.

⅔ cup vegetable oil, plus more for greasing

1⅔ cups all-purpose flour

1 teaspoon ground cinnamon

1 teaspoon baking soda

½ teaspoon fine sea salt

4 teaspoons hemp hearts or seeds, plus ¼ cup for sprinkling

4 teaspoons ground flaxseed meal

2 teaspoons white or black chia seeds

⅔ cup mashed very ripe bananas (2 medium)

½ cup sugar

½ cup coconut sugar or lightly packed dark brown sugar

2 large eggs

Preheat the oven to 350°F. Grease a 12-cup cupcake pan or line with paper liners.

In a large bowl, sift together the flour, cinnamon, baking soda, and salt, then whisk in the hemp, flax, and chia seeds.

In the bowl of a stand mixer fitted with the paddle attachment, beat the bananas, both sugars, oil, and eggs. Add the flour mixture to the banana mixture in two additions, beating until blended after each addition.

Divide the batter among the wells of the prepared pan and sprinkle each muffin generously with 1 teaspoon of hemp hearts. Bake until golden brown and a toothpick inserted into the center comes out clean, 18 to 20 minutes. Transfer the pan to a wire rack and cool completely.

CHOCOLATE CHAI QUICK BREAD WITH CARDAMOM CINNAMON FROSTING

MAKES 2 LOAVES

I'm really a dessert purist at heart, often skeptical of blending a hodgepodge of flavors in the name of "fusion." But after tasting a chai-chocolate bar a few years back, I was made a believer; there is something about combining those two elements that really works! This cake owes its intense spicy notes to chai tea bags, which I steep in advance to infuse the chocolate cake with extra depth. I then top it with a surprising frosting, the flavors of which—cardamom, in particular—both stand up to and complement the chocolate.

½ cup (1 stick) unsalted butter, plus more for greasing

2¼ cups all-purpose flour, plus more for flouring the pans

1 cup boiling water

2 chai tea bags

1½ teaspoons ground cinnamon

1 teaspoon ground ginger

¼ teaspoon ground cardamom

⅛ teaspoon ground cloves

2 teaspoons baking soda

½ teaspoon fine sea salt

1 cup full-fat sour cream

1 teaspoon pure vanilla extract

3 ounces bittersweet chocolate, chopped

2 cups lightly packed dark brown sugar

3 large eggs

Cardamom Cinnamon Frosting

Preheat the oven to 350°F. Butter and flour two 8½ x 4½-inch loaf pans; tap out the excess flour.

In a microwave-safe bowl, pour the boiling water over the tea bags and let the tea steep for at least 10 minutes and up to 1 hour. Remove, squeeze out, and discard the tea bags, reserving the tea.

In a medium bowl, sift together the flour, cinnamon, ginger, cardamom, cloves, baking soda, and salt. In a small bowl, whisk together the sour cream and vanilla. In a microwave-safe bowl, microwave the chocolate on high for 2 to 3 minutes, stopping and stirring every 45 seconds until melted.

In the bowl of a stand mixer fitted with the paddle attachment, beat the butter and brown sugar on high speed until light and fluffy, 2 to 3 minutes. Reduce the speed to low and beat in the eggs one

CARDAMOM CINNAMON FROSTING

MAKES 2 CUPS

3 cups confectioners' sugar

1 teaspoon ground cinnamon

¾ teaspoon ground ginger

½ teaspoon fine sea salt

¼ teaspoon ground cardamom

6 tablespoons (3 ounces) cream cheese, slightly softened

6 tablespoons unsalted butter, slightly softened

2 tablespoons whole milk

In a medium bowl, sift together the confectioners' sugar, cinnamon, ginger, salt, and cardamom.

In the bowl of a stand mixer fitted with the paddle attachment, beat the cream cheese and butter on medium speed until light and fluffy, 2 minutes. Reduce the speed to low, gradually add the confectioners' sugar mixture and milk, and beat until the frosting is creamy and spreadable, 1 to 2 minutes, being careful not to incorporate too much air into the frosting.

at a time, then the melted chocolate, beating after each addition until just blended. Gradually add half the flour mixture, then the sour cream mixture, then the remaining flour mixture, beating after each addition until incorporated. Heat the chai tea in the microwave on high until it boils again, then, while whisking, add it to the batter in a slow stream and whisk until smooth.

Pour the batter into the prepared loaf pans, dividing it evenly, and bake until the tops spring back when pressed and a toothpick inserted into the center comes out clean, 45 to 47 minutes. Transfer the pans to a wire rack and cool for 20 minutes, then tilt the loaves onto the rack and cool completely. Generously frost both loaves with cardamom cinnamon frosting.

SPICED ZUCCHINI BREAD WITH CREAM CHEESE FROSTING

MAKES 2 LOAVES

These fluffy, green-flecked loaves happen to get both sweetness and moisture from an incredible vegetable that can go from "zoodles" to dessert in a single bound. Unlike savory cooking, where zucchini's watery nature can sometimes be problematic, this is a case where that slightly sweet liquid enhances both the flavor and texture of the finished product. Admittedly, there is something sort of sneaky about a cake masquerading as a bread—as if the fact that it's not baked in a round cake pan and stacked in layers makes it more nutritious! Enjoy it . . . and don't worry about the vitamins.

---

1 cup vegetable oil, plus more for greasing

3 cups all-purpose flour

2 teaspoons ground cinnamon

¾ teaspoon ground ginger

½ teaspoon freshly grated nutmeg

¼ teaspoon ground allspice

1 teaspoon fine sea salt

1 teaspoon baking powder

1 teaspoon baking soda

3 large eggs

2¼ cups lightly packed light brown sugar

1 tablespoon pure vanilla extract

2 medium zucchini (10 ounces), grated (3½ cups)

1 cup chopped walnuts

Cream Cheese Frosting (page 14)

Preheat the oven to 325°F. Grease and flour two 8½ x 4½-inch loaf pans; tap out the excess flour.

In a large bowl, sift together the flour, cinnamon, ginger, nutmeg, allspice, salt, baking powder, and baking soda.

In the bowl of a stand mixer fitted with the paddle attachment, beat the eggs, oil, brown sugar, and vanilla on high speed until creamy, 2 to 3 minutes. Reduce the speed to medium-low and add the flour mixture, beating until just blended. Add the zucchini and walnuts and beat until just incorporated.

Divide the batter between the prepared pans and bake until the tops are domed and golden and a toothpick inserted into the center comes out clean, 45 to 50 minutes. Transfer the pans to a wire rack and cool for 20 minutes, then tilt the loaves onto the rack and cool completely. Frost the loaves with cream cheese frosting.

GLAZED LEMON POPPY YOGURT LOAVES

SERVES 8 TO 10

Cakes like these were a favorite treat of mine growing up. I was intrigued by the technique of poking holes into the finished cake, then dousing it in lemon syrup, which allowed the sweet-tart glaze to soak deep inside. Most versions contained sour cream or buttermilk, but I love using Greek yogurt for its mellow tang and thickness. You can also bake these in mini loaf pans, perfect for gift-giving.

½ cup vegetable oil, plus more for greasing

1½ cups all-purpose flour, plus more for flouring the pan

2 teaspoons baking powder

½ teaspoon fine sea salt

1 cup plus 2 tablespoons sugar

3 large eggs

1 cup full-fat plain Greek yogurt

1 tablespoon finely grated lemon zest

½ teaspoon pure vanilla extract

3 tablespoons poppy seeds

1½ tablespoons fresh lemon juice

Preheat the oven to 350°F. Grease and flour an 8½ x 4½-inch loaf pan; tap out the excess flour.

In a medium bowl, sift together the flour, baking powder, and salt. In the bowl of a stand mixer fitted with the paddle attachment, beat the oil and 1 cup of the sugar on medium-high speed until the mixture is fluffy and shaggy, 3 minutes. Add the eggs and beat until creamy, 1 to 2 minutes. Add the yogurt, lemon zest, vanilla, and poppy seeds, lower the speed to medium, and beat until blended, 1 to 2 minutes. Add the dry ingredients and beat until incorporated, 1 minute more. Pour the batter into the prepared pan and bake until a toothpick inserted into the center comes out clean, 55 to 60 minutes. Transfer the pan to a wire rack and cool for 20 minutes, then tilt the loaf onto the rack and cool completely.

Meanwhile, in a small saucepan, bring the lemon juice and remaining 2 tablespoons sugar to a high simmer and simmer until the mixture is clear and the sugar has dissolved, 2 to 3 minutes. Remove from the heat and cool. Set the cake on the wire rack over a baking sheet. Poke holes across the top of the cake with a toothpick and slowly pour the lemon-sugar mixture over the top. Let it cool completely before slicing and serving.

CHAPTER 9

PIES & TARTS

I have to admit, I used to be a little intimidated by pies. Not the eating part...just the making part! My path to pie making was rocky. Always one to worry about overworking the dough, I often ended up with scraggly pastry that cracked and resisted rolling into a smooth, beautiful circle. The perfectionist in me was relentless, attempting new methods and recipes and working on my rolling and crimping technique until, at last, I was satisfied.

In this chapter, I share with you my incredible master pie dough, as well as the tips I have found that help me master what can be a temperamental pastry. Once you bite into that fresh flaky pie, all the work, waiting, and rolling will be worthwhile. There are also a couple of tarts and a gorgeous galette, all with a fresh fruit element, that focus as much on the artistry of presentation as the preparation itself. They're so beautiful it may be hard to take the first bite...but once you do, all bets are off!

LEMON MERINGUE PIE

SERVES 8

There's nothing sunnier than a slice of lemon meringue pie. That bright, cheery lemon curd sitting underneath a billowy cloud of toasty meringue actually takes me back to a time when retro diners and classic Americana ruled the day. And by intensifying the tartness of the lemon curd to counterbalance that sweet, creamy meringue, I gave the original recipe a more modern twist.

While there is a good amount of debate regarding the ideal temperature for layering the meringue on top of the curd, for me, room temperature filling and meringue yield the most seamless results and minimize the amount of "weeping" you sometimes get when the meringue releases liquid. Just make sure the meringue completely envelops the curd to the edges of the pie, then style it into fabulous peaks before baking for full dramatic effect.

FOR THE LEMON FILLING:

4 large egg yolks (save the whites for the meringue)

1 cup plus 2 tablespoons sugar

5 tablespoons cornstarch

⅛ teaspoon fine sea salt

1 cup cold water

½ cup half-and-half

2 tablespoons unsalted butter

2 tablespoons finely grated lemon zest

6 tablespoons fresh lemon juice

FOR THE MERINGUE:

4 large egg whites

¼ teaspoon cream of tartar

½ cup superfine or granulated sugar

½ recipe Master Pie Crust (page 214), blind baked

MAKE THE LEMON FILLING:

In a medium bowl, whisk the egg yolks. In a nonreactive medium saucepan, whisk together the sugar, cornstarch, and salt. Stir in the water and half-and-half and cook over medium heat, stirring frequently, until the mixture just starts to boil, 5 to 6 minutes.

Temper the egg yolks by whisking in a few tablespoons of the hot sugar mixture, 1 tablespoon at a time, then slowly add the tempered yolks back to the saucepan, whisking briskly. Reduce the heat to medium-low and cook until large bubbles form on the surface and the mixture is thick and glossy like pudding, 3 minutes.

Strain through a fine-mesh sieve into a bowl, pushing the mixture through with a wooden spoon or silicone spatula. Whisk in the butter until just melted, then whisk in the lemon zest and juice. Cover with plastic wrap, pressing it directly against the surface of the filling to prevent a skin from forming.

MAKE THE MERINGUE:

Wipe the bowl and whisk attachment of a stand mixer with vinegar to eliminate any grease. Beat the egg whites and cream of tartar on medium speed until foamy, 1 to 2 minutes. Add the sugar 1 tablespoon at a time, increase the speed to high, and whip until the whites form medium peaks and are smooth and shiny, 3 to 4 minutes.

ASSEMBLE AND BAKE THE PIE:

Preheat the oven to 400°F. Remove the plastic wrap from the filling and pour the filling into the baked pie shell. Smooth the top with an offset spatula, then spread the meringue over the top, sealing it completely and creating decorative peaks with a knife or offset spatula. Bake until the meringue is light brown, rotating halfway through, 8 to 9 minutes. Cool on a wire rack to room temperature before serving, about 2 hours.

RED GRAPE MASCARPONE & PISTACHIO TART

SERVES 8

The elegance and sophistication of this tart belie the ease of its preparation. I often find myself whipping it up when I want an impressive-but-easy, presentation-worthy last course for guests. Beautiful green pistachios are ground and blended with a few simple ingredients to form a unique crust. After baking, I fill it with a dreamy mascarpone-enriched cream, then top with glazed red grapes to create a not-too-sweet dinner party dessert that is sure to please. The shimmering grapes' gorgeous color makes for a fresh and festive tart that can even be enjoyed in the heart of winter.

FOR THE PISTACHIO CRUST:

⅓ cup unsalted shelled pistachios

6 tablespoons (¾ stick) unsalted butter, cut into cubes

⅓ cup sugar

½ teaspoon fine sea salt

¾ cup all-purpose flour

FOR THE MASCARPONE FILLING:

¾ cup (6 ounces) mascarpone cheese

3 tablespoons honey

1 teaspoon pure vanilla extract

1 cup heavy cream

1½ cups red grapes, halved

3 tablespoons grape jelly

2 tablespoons boiling water

MAKE THE PISTACHIO CRUST:

In a food processor, pulse the pistachios until finely ground. Add the butter, sugar, and salt and pulse until combined, 10 pulses. Add the flour and pulse until incorporated and the dough is crumbly, 10 pulses. Transfer the dough to a 9-inch fluted tart or round pan with a removable bottom. Using the bottom of a glass, press the dough all over the bottom and up the sides of the pan. Refrigerate until chilled, 30 minutes.

Preheat the oven to 300°F. Prick the dough all over with a fork and bake until fragrant, 25 minutes. Transfer to a rack and cool completely.

(Continued)

MAKE THE MASCARPONE FILLING:

In a small bowl, whisk together the mascarpone, honey, and vanilla until smooth.

In the bowl of a stand mixer fitted with the whisk attachment, whip the cream on medium speed until soft peaks form, 2 to 3 minutes. Reduce the speed to medium-low, add the mascarpone mixture, and continue to whip until firm peaks form (this will happen fast, so be careful not to overwhip), 30 seconds. Scrape the filling into the cooled crust and refrigerate until set, 2 hours.

Working from the outside, arrange the grape halves cut-side down in the pattern of your choice over the top of the tart. Just before serving, in a small saucepan over medium-low heat, or in a small glass bowl in the microwave, gently heat the jelly and water, 1 to 2 minutes, whisking to unify, then brush over the grapes.

SWEET CHERRY PIE

SERVES 8

One thing I've learned as a professional baker is that the best ingredients aren't always what you expect. Though I love fresh cherries, their season is so short; for that reason, I recommend using frozen cherries here. Not only are they frozen at the peak of freshness, but they're pitted, eliminating an extra step when you just want to get this delicious pie into the oven! A squeeze of fresh lemon delivers a citrusy accent that perfectly complements the cherries' sweetness.

2½ pounds (7 cups) frozen dark sweet cherries, partially thawed, any juice reserved

¼ cup cornstarch

1 cup plus 2 tablespoons sugar

2 teaspoons finely grated lemon zest (from 1 large lemon)

1 tablespoon fresh lemon juice

¼ teaspoon fine sea salt

Flour, for dusting

1 recipe Master Pie Crust (page 214), dough chilled

1 egg white, beaten

Preheat the oven to 375°F. Line a rimmed baking sheet with parchment paper. Place the cherries in a large saucepan and heat over medium-low heat until the cherries release their liquid and soften, 15 minutes, using a potato masher or large wooden spoon to partially mash the cherries (you should still be able to see large chunks of cherry). Turn off the heat and drain the liquid into a bowl, adding any reserved thawing liquid; reserve the cherries. Add the cornstarch to the liquid and whisk well until completely dissolved, adding 1 tablespoon of water if necessary. Add the sugar to the cherries and cook over low heat, stirring, until the sugar has dissolved. Add the cornstarch mixture and stir continuously until no visible lumps remain and the mixture is thickened and glossy, 7 to 8 minutes. Remove from the heat and stir in the lemon zest and juice and the salt. Transfer to a bowl to cool until ready to use.

Remove one disc of dough from the refrigerator. On a lightly floured surface using a lightly floured rolling pin, roll out the dough, rotating and carefully flipping the dough, sprinkling flour lightly on the dough as needed, until you have a 12-inch round (the dough should be smooth and not sticky). Carefully roll the dough back over the rolling pin and drape it over a 9-inch glass pie pan, gently guiding the dough into the plate. Trim the dough, leaving a ½-inch overhang all around the pie pan. Chill the bottom crust while you make the lattice. On a lightly floured surface, roll out the other pie disc to a 13-inch diameter. Using a sharp knife or pastry wheel, cut the dough into eight ¾- to 1-inch-wide strips.

Remove the bottom crust from the refrigerator and pour the filling into the pie. Arrange the dough strips across the pie, leaving about ¾ of an inch between each strip. Fold every other dough strip back in half onto itself and place one piece of dough across and just underneath the strips that have been folded back. Unfold the strips back over the new strip. Fold the strips lying under the perpendicular strip up upon themselves, just like you did before, then arrange another long strip down and unfold the strips over it. Repeat with the remaining strips using this weaving method until you have a lattice crust. Trim the top strips flush with the bottom crust, then fold the overhanging bottom crust over the strips and crimp into a decorative pattern. Carefully brush the lattice and edges with the egg white.

Place on a baking sheet and bake until the juices are bubbling and the crust is golden brown, 1 hour, protecting the crust edges with aluminum foil or a crust shield if they begin to get too dark. Cool on a wire rack for 4 hours, or up to overnight, to allow the filling to thicken before serving.

MOM'S SHATTER-TOP MIXED BERRY CRISP

SERVES 6

My mother has always been famous for her spectacular dinner parties, and her even more elaborate and indulgent desserts. These days, though she still wows her guests with a show-stopping finish, it's often of a slightly lighter variety. I've taken a cue from her, preparing some of her classics—like this berry crisp—with fresh fruit and whole wheat flour. A touch of all-purpose flour binds the fruit's natural juices, forming a luscious layer underneath. A shallow baking dish makes for a stellar crust-to-fruit ratio, and the "crisp" itself forms a shell-like top that you crack through with a firm tap of your spoon. For an added treat, serve warm with vanilla ice cream.

FOR THE FRUIT FILLING:

Butter, for greasing

1½ pounds mixed berries (about 5 cups), such as blackberries, blueberries, raspberries, and/or halved hulled strawberries

⅓ cup lightly packed dark brown sugar

¼ cup all-purpose flour

FOR THE CRISP TOPPING:

⅓ cup all-purpose flour

⅓ cup whole wheat pastry flour

⅔ cup sugar

¾ teaspoon baking powder

½ teaspoon fine sea salt

1 large egg white

4 tablespoons (½ stick) unsalted butter, melted

Vanilla ice cream, for serving (optional)

MAKE THE FRUIT FILLING:

Preheat the oven to 350°F. Lightly butter a 9-inch round or square glass or ceramic baking dish. In a large bowl, combine berries, brown sugar, and flour and gently toss until evenly coated. Transfer to the prepared baking dish.

MAKE THE TOPPING:

In a large bowl, whisk together the all-purpose and whole wheat flours, sugar, baking powder, and salt. Form a well in the center of the dry ingredients, add the egg white, and stir with a fork until the mixture becomes crumbly and has the consistency of bread crumbs. Sprinkle the topping evenly over the fruit, drizzle the melted butter evenly over the entire surface, and bake until the topping is golden and crisp and the fruit is bubbling at the sides, 35 to 38 minutes. Cool slightly and serve warm or at room temperature, with vanilla ice cream, if desired.

GRAPEFRUIT CURD TART WITH GINGERSNAP CRUST

SERVES 8

I adore using pink grapefruit in desserts. It delivers the same tart, acidic flavor as lemon or lime, but with the added benefit of a beautiful rosy hue and a touch of natural sweetness. One of my favorite recipes in the book, my Spicy Gingersnap Cookies (page 123), serves as the base of the tart crust. The crunch and peppery spice of the cookies play beautifully against the grapefruit's refreshingly sweet-sour curd. Decorate the top with grapefruit segments for a juicy bite and pretty presentation.

FOR THE GINGERSNAP CRUST:

12 baked Spicy Gingersnap Cookies (page 123)

2 tablespoons unsalted butter, melted

2 tablespoons sugar

1 tablespoon turbinado sugar, such as Sugar In The Raw

1 tablespoon cornstarch

2 teaspoons water

⅛ teaspoon fine sea salt

FOR THE GRAPEFRUIT CURD:

1½ cups fresh pink or red grapefruit juice (from 2 large grapefruits), strained of any excess pulp

6 large eggs

4 large egg yolks

½ cup sugar

⅛ teaspoon fine sea salt

½ cup (1 stick) unsalted butter, softened, cut into pieces

2 tablespoons finely grated grapefruit zest

1 large, ripe pink grapefruit

MAKE THE GINGERSNAP CRUST:

Preheat the oven to 300°F. Arrange the already-baked cookies on a baking sheet and bake until fragrant, 6 to 7 minutes; cool completely.

In a food processor, process the twice-baked gingersnap cookies into fine crumbs, 45 seconds to 1 minute (you should have 1½ cups of crumbs). Add the butter, both sugars, cornstarch, water, and salt and pulse until the mixture holds together when pinched between your fingers, 25 to 30 pulses. Press into the bottom and up the sides of a 9-inch tart pan with a removable bottom and bake until the crust is golden and set, 12 to 13 minutes. Transfer the pan to a wire rack and cool completely.

MAKE THE GRAPEFRUIT CURD:

In a small (2-quart) saucepan, bring the grapefruit juice to a boil, then reduce the heat to medium-high and cook until the juice has reduced to ½ cup, pouring the liquid into a measuring cup every 5 minutes to check the amount, for 15 to 20 minutes. Remove from the heat and cool to room temperature in the saucepan, 30 minutes.

MAKE THE CUSTARD AND ASSEMBLE THE TART:

In a medium saucepan, whisk together the eggs, egg yolks, sugar, and salt, then whisk in the reduced grapefruit juice a little at a time and bring to a simmer over medium-low heat, whisking and dropping the butter into the mixture in small pieces until the curd thickens and coats the back of a spoon, 8 to 9 minutes. Do not let the mixture boil or the curd may curdle. Remove from the heat and press through a fine-mesh sieve with a wooden spoon or silicone spatula into a medium bowl. Stir in the zest, then cover with plastic wrap, pressing it directly against the surface of the curd to prevent a skin from forming, and cool for 15 minutes. Pour the curd into the cooled crust, smooth the top with an offset spatula, and chill until set, 2 hours.

Using a serrated knife, cut the skin away from the grapefruit, then cut the grapefruit between the membranes into segments. Arrange the segments on a paper towel–lined plate to soak up any additional juice, then refrigerate to firm. Arrange the grapefruit segments on top of the tart in a decorative pattern, release the tart from the sides of the pan, and transfer to a serving plate.

CHOCOLATE BOURBON PECAN PIE

SERVES 8

A pecan pie is a thing of beauty, but I wanted to find a new way to add some complexity and sophistication to the classic. Instead of a typical jelly-like filling to hold the pecans, I add dark corn syrup and two kinds of chocolate, then spike it with bourbon to take this rich, nut-studded dessert over the top. This pie can be made the day before serving, and, if you like, you can leave out the bourbon and increase the vanilla by one tablespoon.

2 ounces unsweetened chocolate, coarsely chopped

⅓ cup unsalted butter

¼ cup unsweetened cocoa powder

¾ cup sugar

¾ cup dark corn syrup

½ teaspoon fine sea salt

3 large eggs

1 large egg yolk

3 tablespoons bourbon

1 teaspoon pure vanilla extract

1½ cups pecan halves

½ recipe Master Pie Crust (page 214), blind baked

⅓ cup bittersweet or semisweet chocolate chips

Sweet Whipped Cream (page 68)

Preheat the oven to 325°F.

In a microwave-safe bowl, microwave the chocolate and butter on high for 2 to 3 minutes, stopping and stirring every 45 seconds until melted. Whisk together until smooth, then add the cocoa powder and whisk until smooth. Whisk in the sugar, corn syrup, salt, eggs, egg yolk, bourbon, and vanilla until smooth. Sprinkle 1 cup of the pecans evenly across the bottom of the blind-baked crust and slowly pour in the filling in a spiral motion, working from the inside out. Sprinkle the chocolate chips evenly over the top of the pie, then arrange the remaining pecans on top of the chocolate chip layer in a decorative pattern. Place the pie on a baking sheet and bake until the center of the pie has puffed and the filling jiggles only slightly when the pan is gently shaken, about 45 minutes. Transfer to a wire rack and cool for several hours before cutting and serving with whipped cream.

CARAMEL LACQUERED APPLE PIE

SERVES 8

I found a way to improve upon the old-fashioned cupcake, so I knew there had to be a way to spruce up this classic! Though at first glance apple pie seems a fairly straightforward dessert, there are actually a million ways for it to go wrong, including apples that come out crunchy even after an hour of baking. The secret lies in precooking the apples before baking, which makes them tender and flavorful. To further improve on the original, I created a buttery caramel sauce that gets added to the cooked apples *and* brushed right on top during baking (you'll have leftover sauce, but I'm sure you'll figure out plenty of ways to enjoy it). The caramel on the crust creates a deeply burnished, lacquered effect that's as magical to look at as it is to taste.

FOR THE SALTED CARAMEL SAUCE:

½ cup (1 stick) unsalted butter

½ cup sugar

½ cup lightly packed light brown sugar

½ cup light corn syrup

¾ cup heavy cream

1 teaspoon pure vanilla extract

½ teaspoon fine sea salt

FOR THE APPLE PIE FILLING:

2 tablespoons unsalted butter

8 large Golden Delicious apples (about 4 pounds), peeled, cored, and sliced into ½-inch wedges

¼ teaspoon kosher salt

¾ cup lightly packed light brown sugar

1½ tablespoons all-purpose flour

1½ tablespoons cornstarch

1 tablespoon fresh lemon juice

Flour, for dusting

1 recipe Master Pie Crust (page 214), dough chilled

1 large egg

MAKE THE SALTED CARAMEL SAUCE:

In a heavy-bottomed medium saucepan, combine the butter, both sugars, corn syrup, and heavy cream and bring to a boil over medium-high heat. Cook, whisking occasionally, until the sugar has fully dissolved and the mixture begins to bubble. Reduce the heat to medium and simmer (the surface will be bubbling), stirring occasionally, until the caramel is thickened, golden brown, and coats the back of a spoon, 9 minutes. Remove from the heat and stir in the vanilla and salt (the sauce may not seem thick enough, but it will thicken as it cools).

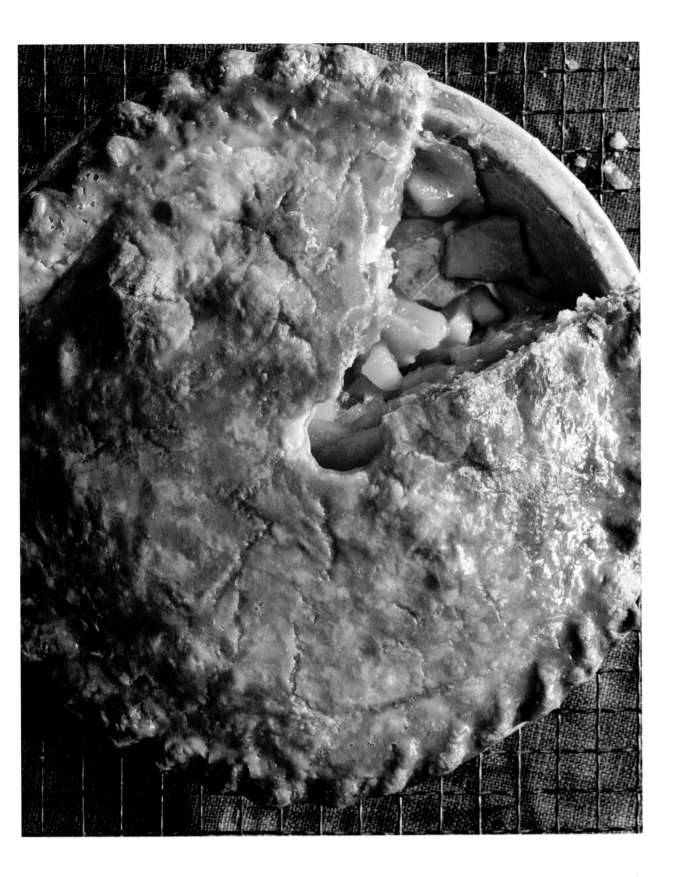

MAKE THE APPLE PIE FILLING:

In a large skillet, melt the butter over medium-high heat. Add the apples and cook, stirring, until coated with the butter. Sprinkle the salt and brown sugar over the pan, stirring to combine as the apples begin to release their liquid. Reduce the heat to medium and simmer until the apples have started to soften, 5 to 6 minutes. Sprinkle the flour and cornstarch over the apples and cook, stirring occasionally, until the liquid has thickened and coats the apples, 1 to 2 minutes more (the apples will be silky, slightly limp, and soft, but not mushy). Remove the pan from the heat, add the lemon juice, stir to incorporate, and scrape the fruit mixture into a bowl or onto a baking sheet to cool completely.

BAKE THE PIE:

Arrange a rack in the center of the oven and preheat the oven to 425°F. Cover a large baking sheet with aluminum foil and set it on the oven rack.

On a lightly floured surface using a lightly floured rolling pin, roll out the dough, rotating and carefully flipping the dough and sprinkling it lightly with flour as needed, until you have a 12-inch round (the dough should be smooth and not sticky). Carefully roll the dough back over the rolling pin and drape it over a 9-inch glass pie pan, gently guiding the dough into the plate. Trim the dough, leaving a ½-inch overhang all around the pie pan. Chill in the refrigerator while you roll out the other disc of dough. On a lightly floured surface, roll out the other disc of dough to a 13-inch diameter. Remove the chilled pie crust from the refrigerator and pour ¼ cup of the caramel sauce evenly over the bottom of the dough (if the caramel sauce has been refrigerated, warm it in the microwave for 1 minute to loosen). Place the cooled pie filling on top and drizzle another ¼ cup of the caramel sauce over the filling. Cover with the second crust, trim the excess with a paring knife, and fold the dough under itself around the edges to seal. Crimp the edges with the tines of a fork or with your fingers into a decorative pattern. Using a sharp knife, cut three or four steam vents in the top crust. Whisk the egg with 2 teaspoons water and lightly brush the top of the pie with the egg wash.

Bake the pie on the hot baking sheet for 20 minutes, then reduce the oven temperature to 375°F and bake for 20 minutes more. Remove the pie from the oven, brush with 2 tablespoons of the caramel sauce, and return to the oven, rotated 180 degrees from its original direction. Bake until the interior is bubbling and the crust is golden brown and shiny, 15 to 20 minutes more.

Transfer the pan to a wire rack and cool for at least 2 hours before serving. Serve with the remaining caramel sauce, or store the sauce in an airtight container in the fridge for up to 1 month for another use.

PEACH & BLACKBERRY GALETTE

SERVES 8

I love the simple, rustic elegance of a galette, which envelops peak-season fruit in a free-form crust. Unlike a pie, which I always feel a little bit of pressure to make look perfect, a galette is *meant* to be just a little more forgiving in construction and appearance; once baked, the crust forms a beautiful frame around the juicy fruit. I use a combination of all-purpose and whole wheat flours in the dough, which lends a slight nuttiness without sacrificing its tender bite.

* If it's not peach season or you can't find juicy, ripe peaches, by all means use a 1-pound bag of frozen, partially defrosted peaches (slice them into ½-inch-thick slices if they're wider).

FOR THE GALETTE DOUGH:

1 cup all-purpose flour, plus more for dusting

½ cup whole wheat flour or whole wheat pastry flour

4 teaspoons sugar

⅛ teaspoon fine sea salt

10 tablespoons (1¼ sticks) cold unsalted butter, cut into ½-inch pieces

⅓ cup very cold heavy cream, plus more as needed

FOR THE FRUIT FILLING:

⅔ cup sugar

¼ cup cornstarch

1¼ pounds ripe peaches* (4 or 5 medium), sliced into ¼-inch wedges (about 3 cups)

1 cup fresh blackberries

1 teaspoon finely grated lemon zest

2 tablespoons fresh lemon juice

1 vanilla bean, halved lengthwise and seeds scraped

FOR FINISHING AND BAKING:

1 tablespoon heavy cream

1 tablespoon turbinado or granulated sugar

MAKE THE GALETTE DOUGH:

In a food processor, pulse the flours, sugar, and salt until incorporated, about 5 pulses. Add the butter and pulse until incorporated but still with lots of visible pea-size pieces, 10 to 15 pulses (make sure not to overprocess). Add the cream and pulse until the mixture is moistened but still clumpy and not fully unified, 10 to 15 more pulses. (If the dough feels too dry and does not stick together between your fingers, add more cream by the teaspoon until you achieve a sticky texture.) Transfer the dough to a floured work surface and gently gather it into a ball. Form a 6 x 1-inch disc out of the dough, wrap tightly in plastic wrap, and refrigerate until firm, at least 2 hours and up to 24.

(Continued)

MAKE THE FRUIT FILLING:

In a large bowl, whisk together the sugar and cornstarch. Add the peaches, blackberries, lemon zest and juice, and vanilla bean seeds and toss gently to combine.

SHAPE, FINISH, AND BAKE THE GALETTE:

Preheat the oven to 400°F.

Unwrap the dough, flour it gently on both sides, place it in between two pieces of parchment paper, and let it sit for 3 minutes to soften slightly. Roll out the dough into a 13-inch round, transfer to an unrimmed baking sheet, and chill until ready to use.

Remove the top layer of parchment from the dough. Using a slotted spoon, transfer the fruit from the bowl and mound it in the center of the dough, leaving a 1½- to 2-inch border uncovered. Fold the pastry border over the fruit, creating a thick layer to hold the fruit in (the folded dough will overlap in a few places; press the dough together in those spots). Drizzle ¼ cup of the liquid from the fruit bowl on top of the fruit, discarding the rest. Brush the dough generously with the cream and sprinkle with the turbinado sugar.

Bake until the crust is golden and the filling is bubbling, 40 to 42 minutes (some liquid may ooze out—this is okay!). Transfer the pan to a wire rack and cool to room temperature, at least 30 minutes. Using a cake lifter or two large spatulas, gently transfer the galette to a serving plate.

CHOCOLATE-CRUSTED PUMPKIN PIE

SERVES 8

Every year I pull the same fiercely protected, tried-and-true recipes out of my Thanksgiving file, then set to work in the kitchen creating the traditional dishes my family looks forward to all year. I'm hesitant to mess with them for sentimental reasons, so I was slightly uneasy about serving my new riff on our beloved pumpkin pie recipe: A chocolate crust? Madness! It's a delicious surprise that manages to make that luscious pumpkin flavor pop even more! Luckily, just as I became completely smitten, my family gave it their Turkey Day approval!

FOR THE GRAHAM CRUST:

3 cups Chocolate Teddy Grahams cookies

6 tablespoons (¾ stick) unsalted butter, melted

FOR THE PUMPKIN FILLING:

1 (15-ounce) can pure pumpkin puree (not pumpkin pie filling)

½ cup heavy cream

¼ cup sweetened condensed milk

2 large eggs

½ cup lightly packed light brown sugar

¼ cup sugar

1 tablespoon pure vanilla extract or bourbon

1½ teaspoons ground cinnamon

1 teaspoon ground ginger

½ teaspoon ground allspice

¼ teaspoon freshly grated nutmeg

¼ teaspoon ground cloves

⅛ teaspoon fine sea salt

Sweet Whipped Cream (page 68)

MAKE THE GRAHAM CRUST:

In a food processor, pulse to break up the cookies, then process until fine, 30 seconds. Drizzle in the butter and pulse until coated and the crust holds together when pinched between your fingers. Press into a 9-inch pie pan and chill.

MAKE THE PUMPKIN FILLING:

Preheat the oven to 400°F. In a large bowl, whisk together the pumpkin, cream, condensed milk, eggs, both sugars, vanilla, cinnamon, ginger, allspice, nutmeg, cloves, and salt. Pour the filling into the prepared crust and bake for 15 minutes. Reduce the oven temperature to 350°F and bake until just set (the center will still be slightly jiggly), 35 to 40 minutes more. Transfer the pan to a wire rack and cool completely. Serve with whipped cream.

MALTED CHOCOLATE PUDDING PIE

SERVES 8

My mom's love of malt began with Cho-Chos, a frozen treat sold from ice cream trucks in the 1950s. She passed that passion firmly along to me, reinforcing our shared adoration with trips to ice cream parlors for malted sundaes and milk shakes. Though malt is a bit of a forgotten flavor these days, it still has the ability to turn a common dessert into something extraordinary. My silky chocolate pudding is the perfect vehicle for this special malt flavor; the form here is simple vanilla malt powder you can find in virtually any supermarket, often in the ice cream department or close to the condensed and evaporated milk. Matched with a flaky, buttery crust and lightly sweetened cream, this "oldie but goodie" is part of my plan to transfer my family's malt madness on to the next generation!

4 large egg yolks

¾ cup sugar

⅓ cup cornstarch

⅛ teaspoon fine sea salt

⅓ cup malted milk powder, such as Carnation brand

2 cups heavy cream

1¾ cups whole milk

3 ounces semisweet chocolate, chopped

3 tablespoons unsalted butter

2 teaspoons pure vanilla extract

½ Master Pie Crust recipe (page 214), blind baked

Sweet Whipped Cream (Page 68)

Preheat the oven to 400°F.

In a medium bowl, whisk the egg yolks. In a small bowl, whisk together the sugar, cornstarch, salt, and malted milk powder.

In a medium saucepan, whisk together the cream and milk and heat over medium-low heat until warmed, 2 to 3 minutes. While whisking, add the sugar mixture and bring to a simmer.

Temper the egg yolks by whisking in a third of the hot sugar mixture, 1 tablespoon at a time, then slowly add the tempered yolks back to the saucepan, whisking briskly. Reduce the heat to medium-low and cook until large bubbles form on the surface and the mixture is thick and glossy like pudding, 3 minutes.

Raise the heat to medium-high and bring the pudding to a boil for 30 seconds, whisking continuously. Remove from the heat and strain through a fine-mesh sieve into a bowl, pushing the pudding through with a wooden spoon or silicone spatula. Whisk in the chocolate, butter, and vanilla until smooth, then cover with plastic wrap,

pressing it directly against the surface of the pudding to prevent a skin from forming, and cool for 15 minutes.

Remove the plastic from the pudding and pour it into the baked pie shell. Smooth the top with an offset spatula, then refrigerate for at least 4 to 6 hours or up to overnight. When ready to serve, top the pie with whipped cream.

BANANA CREAM PIE

SERVES 8

When Charles was growing up in Oklahoma, his Aunt Kathy—who isn't Charles's relative by birth, but rather a friend so close she long ago became an unofficial "aunt"—would make him this silky, pudding-filled pie, satisfying a wicked sweet tooth that has carried into his adult life (trust me!). He still requests it to this day, and when he goes back home to see family, one of these inevitably materializes.

Inspired by Aunt Kathy's recipe—which uses a pastry-crust base and is perfection in its own right—I created a graham-crusted version I hope will become a new classic. Infusing the cream with fresh bananas gives the pudding an extra dimension; the longer you let the bananas steep, the better.

FOR THE GRAHAM CRUST:

10 whole graham crackers (20 squares)

¼ cup sugar

½ teaspoon ground cinnamon

6 tablespoons (¾ stick) unsalted butter, melted

FOR THE BANANA FILLING:

5 ripe medium bananas (about 2 pounds, unpeeled)

2½ cups half-and-half

½ cup sugar

6 large egg yolks

¼ teaspoon fine sea salt

3 tablespoons cornstarch

2 tablespoons unsalted butter

1½ teaspoons pure vanilla extract

1 tablespoon fresh lemon juice

Sweet Whipped Cream (page 68), for topping

MAKE THE GRAHAM CRUST:

Preheat the oven to 375°F.

In a food processor, process the graham crackers, sugar, and cinnamon until fine crumbs form, 30 seconds. Transfer the mixture to a bowl, add the melted butter, and stir until evenly coated (the crumbs should hold together when pressed between your fingers; if not, add water 1 teaspoon at a time until the crumbs hold together). Press the crumbs into the bottom and up the sides of a 9-inch pie pan and bake until dry and set, 8 to 9 minutes. Transfer the pan to a wire rack and cool completely.

(Continued)

MAKE THE FILLING:

Peel and slice two of the bananas into ¼-inch rounds and place them in a heavy-bottomed saucepan. Add the half-and-half and bring to a boil for 1 minute. Remove from the heat, cool for 30 minutes, cover, and chill, letting the mixture steep for 1 hour and up to 24 hours (the longer you steep, the more intense the banana flavor). Strain into a bowl and discard the bananas.

In a medium saucepan, off the heat, whisk together the sugar, egg yolks, and salt until smooth, then whisk in the cornstarch. Add the banana-infused half-and-half, whisking briskly. Cook over medium heat, whisking continuously, until thickened and bubbling but not fully set, 6 to 7 minutes. Remove from the heat and whisk in the butter and vanilla until smooth. Using a silicone spatula or wooden spoon, push the custard through a fine-mesh sieve into a bowl and cool, stirring every few minutes, until just warm, 10 to 15 minutes.

FILL AND TOP THE PIE:

Slice the remaining three bananas into ¼-inch rounds and toss with the lemon juice. Pour a little less than half (about ¾ cup) of the warm filling into the prepared crust, then arrange two-thirds of the sliced bananas on top of the filling. Top with the remaining custard, then arrange the remaining sliced bananas on top of the custard. Cover with plastic wrap, pressing it directly against the surface of the pie, and refrigerate until chilled and set, 4 to 5 hours. Remove from the refrigerator and remove the plastic wrap. Top with whipped cream.

MASTER PIE CRUST

The recipe makes enough dough for either a two-crust pie (top and bottom crusts) or two single-crust pies (just bottom crusts). If you only require one, you can make half the recipe in the small bowl of a food processor or using a handheld pastry blender.

2½ cups all-purpose flour

1½ teaspoons sugar

1 teaspoon fine sea salt

1 cup (2 sticks) unsalted butter, cut into ½-inch cubes, chilled in the freezer for 20 minutes

½ cup ice water, plus more as needed

In a food processor, pulse the flour, sugar, and salt until incorporated, about 5 pulses. Add the butter and pulse until incorporated but still with lots of visible pea-size pieces, 10 to 15 pulses (make sure not to overprocess). Add ¼ cup of the ice water and pulse the dough, then add the remaining ¼ cup water, 1 tablespoon at a time, pulsing after each addition, until the dough just comes together and small pieces of butter are still visible; be careful not to overwork the dough. Divide the dough in half and form each half into a 5 x 1-inch disc. Wrap each disc in plastic wrap and chill for at least 30 minutes before using.

MASTERING PIE CRUST

At the heart of every great pie is a great crust. I wanted mine to work in a variety of recipes, be a snap to make, and be easy to work with. This one fits the bill on all counts! My recipe, adapted from one I found in *Gourmet* magazine many years ago, is a wonder of flakiness and versatility. Once you make it a couple of times, you'll practically have the recipe committed to memory. Here are just a few things to remember:

Cold butter counts! It helps maintain the structure of the dough when it bakes, yielding that characteristic flakiness.

Don't overwork the dough. Processing or kneading too much activates gluten, which makes the dough tough. Follow the instructions closely, making sure not to overdo it.

Look for the lumps. When pulsing the butter into the flour, make sure to leave those pea-size pieces of butter in the mix; when rolled out, they create thin sheets of fat that separate the layers of dough, making a super-flaky crust.

Protecting the edges. Many things can impact how quickly a pie crust browns—especially on its fragile edges. Everything from rack position to the type of filling in the pie can cause the crust to brown too quickly; you can protect your pie by folding aluminum foil over the crust's edges. There are even handy plastic or metal crust "shields" that you can buy for a few dollars, which simply lie over the top of your crust.

Blind baking the crust. When serving a cold pie, such as one filled with lemon curd or pudding, prebaking (or "blind baking") the crust helps ensure that the crust on your finished dessert is fully baked and flaky through and through.

To blind bake, preheat the oven to 375°F.

On a lightly floured surface using a lightly floured rolling pin, roll out the dough, rotating and carefully flipping the dough, sprinkling flour lightly on the dough as needed, until you have a 12-inch round (the dough should be smooth and not sticky). Carefully roll the dough back over the rolling pin and drape it over a 9-inch glass pie pan, gently guiding the dough into the plate. Trim the dough, leaving a ½-inch overhang all around the pie pan. Tuck the overhang underneath itself and use a fork or your fingers to crimp the edges. Using a fork, prick holes in the surface of the dough. Fit a piece of aluminum foil or parchment paper into the pie shell, making sure to cover the bottom and side and fill it with dried beans, uncooked rice, or pie weights to prevent the dough from puffing while baking. Bake until the edges begin to set, 15 minutes. Remove the foil or parchment with the weights and bake until the crust is set and golden, 10 minutes more. Transfer the pan to a wire rack and cool completely.

Use a pastry blender. If you don't have, or feel like using, a food processor, this handheld device, with a thick handle and a curved series of blades underneath—allows you to make pie dough in a few quick motions. To do so, follow the instructions for food processor use, but where it calls for pulsing, use the pastry blender to incorporate the ingredients by hand.

CHAPTER 10

CASUAL CAKES

People sometimes get a little nervous when they bring baked goods to a party I'm attending. Given my role as a cupcake judge on Food Network's *Cupcake Wars*, perhaps they feel like they are under review. Nothing could be further from the truth! I am always quick to assure them that I would never criticize anyone who took the time to bake something on their own. In fact, I always applaud it. It's increasingly rare that we have time to bake from scratch, so it's extra meaningful when we do. Besides, nothing makes people feel more special than someone taking the time to bake from scratch for them, so this chapter is devoted to the types of cakes that you can make "just because." They require no special occasion other than to make people feel good.

DEVIL'S FOOD CAKE

SERVES 8 TO 10

Everyone seems to have a favorite version of devil's food cake, and this is mine. Characterized by rich, not-too-sweet chocolate flavor and incredibly moist texture, it gets an indulgent (and even more chocolaty) lift from the whipped ganache frosting. This cake is also incredibly forgiving; I have left it in the oven a few minutes too long, and it's still great. I have eaten a slice three days after baking . . . still delicious and moist!! It's not magic . . . it's baking science! The generous amount of hot water in the recipe adds moisture to the batter in the most natural way.

Butter, for greasing

1¾ cups all-purpose flour, plus more for flouring the pans

2 cups sugar

⅔ cup unsweetened cocoa powder

1½ teaspoons baking powder

1½ teaspoons baking soda

1 teaspoon fine sea salt

2 large eggs

1 cup whole milk

½ cup vegetable oil

2 teaspoons pure vanilla extract

¾ cup very hot water

Chocolate Ganache Frosting

Preheat the oven to 350°F. Butter two 9-inch round cake pans, line the bottoms with parchment paper cut to fit, and butter the parchment. Flour the pans, coating the bottom and sides of each pan, then tap out the excess flour.

In the bowl of a stand mixer fitted with the paddle attachment, mix the sugar, flour, cocoa powder, baking powder, baking soda, and salt on low speed until combined. In a separate bowl, whisk together the eggs, milk, oil, and vanilla. With the mixer on low speed, slowly add the egg mixture to the flour mixture and beat until blended. Slowly add the hot water, stopping the mixer as soon as the mixture is blended (the batter will be thin). Divide the batter between the prepared pans, place the pans on baking sheets, and bake until the tops are dry and spring back, the sides have pulled away from the pan, and a toothpick inserted into the center comes out clean, 25 to 30 minutes. Cool the cakes completely on a wire rack and then invert them onto cake rounds or onto the wire rack.

Using a long serrated knife, trim off any uneven or domed parts from the top of each cake to create a flat surface. Place one of the

CHOCOLATE GANACHE FROSTING

12 ounces bittersweet chocolate, finely chopped

3 tablespoons unsweetened cocoa powder

3 tablespoons unsalted butter, cut into cubes and slightly softened

1⅔ cups heavy cream

1 teaspoon pure vanilla extract

¼ teaspoon fine sea salt

¾ cup confectioners' sugar, sifted

In the bowl of a stand mixer fitted with the whisk attachment, add the chocolate, cocoa, and butter.

In a small saucepan, heat the cream until very hot but not boiling, then pour it over the chocolate mixture. Wait 2 minutes, then briskly whisk the ingredients until smooth, 15 to 30 seconds. Whisk in the vanilla and salt, then the confectioners' sugar. Chill until the ganache begins to solidify but is not rock hard, 20 to 25 minutes. Switch to the paddle attachment and beat the chilled ganache until it lightens in color, 2 to 3 minutes.

cakes on a serving platter, leveled-side up. Using an offset spatula, frost the top of that layer, then stack the other cake layer on top, leveled part facing down. Create a crumb coat (see page 242) and place remaining frosting on the top of the cake. Working from the center outward, frost the top and the sides of the cake, adding the rest of the frosting as needed.

MICHAEL STRAHAN'S MOM'S BUTTER CAKE

SERVES 12

My friend Sam Phipps first introduced me to Michael Strahan, and it was love at first meeting. Michael is everything he appears to be: down-to-earth, huge-hearted, and a lot of fun. When Sprinkles opened its ice cream store in Manhattan, I asked him if he might want to develop a special flavor, with the proceeds going to benefit St. Jude Children's Research Hospital, a charity near and dear to his heart. Of course he said yes, and—it gets better—he chose to honor his mother and the butter cake she made for him growing up!

The resulting flavor, Mom & Michael's Masterpiece Mix, consisted of vanilla ice cream laced with chocolate-covered peanuts, chocolate chips, and ribbons of caramel. Each scoop was topped with freshly baked cake crumbles inspired by Michael's mother's famous recipe. Super yummy, and it raised lots of money for St. Jude. Win-win!

Another victory here: Michael is sharing his mom's amazing butter cake and chocolate frosting recipe. I took all the great things about boxed vanilla cake mix—a moist crumb and rich flavor—and converted it into an easy, sour cream–enriched, from-scratch recipe. The result is a cake that allows us all to feel like kids again.

½ cup (1 stick) unsalted butter, melted, plus more for greasing

1½ cups all-purpose flour

1½ cups cake flour

4 teaspoons baking powder

½ teaspoon fine sea salt

1 cup full-fat sour cream

2 teaspoons pure vanilla extract

1⅓ cups sugar

½ cup vegetable oil

5 large eggs

Creamy Chocolate Frosting

Preheat the oven to 350°F. Generously butter a 9 x 13-inch baking pan.

In a medium bowl, whisk together the flours, baking powder, and salt. In a small bowl, stir together the sour cream and vanilla.

In the bowl of a stand mixer fitted with the paddle attachment, beat the sugar, butter, and oil on medium speed until fluffy, 2 minutes. Reduce the speed to low and add the eggs one at a time, beating until smooth after each addition, 1 minute. Slowly add one-third of the flour mixture, then half the sour cream mixture, then

CREAMY CHOCOLATE FROSTING

MAKES 3 CUPS

½ cup (1 stick) unsalted butter, slightly softened

3¾ cups confectioners' sugar, sifted

⅓ cup unsweetened cocoa powder, sifted

1 (14-ounce) can evaporated milk

In the bowl of a stand mixer fitted with the paddle attachment, beat the butter on medium speed for 1 minute and then slowly add the confectioners' sugar and cocoa. Gradually add the evaporated milk and beat until the frosting is smooth and creamy, 3 minutes.

half the remaining flour, then the remaining sour cream mixture, and finally the remaining flour, beating after each addition until just blended.

Pour the batter into the prepared pan, spreading it evenly. Bake, turning once halfway through, until the edges brown and a toothpick inserted into the center comes out clean, 25 to 28 minutes.

Cool the cake completely on a wire rack, then use a sharp knife to separate the cake from the pan on all sides. Frost with creamy chocolate frosting.

GINGER-LIME SNACK CAKE

MAKES 20 SQUARES

It goes without saying that I believe in dessert at any hour! The idea that you don't have to wait for a sweet treat but, rather, can eat cake whenever the urge strikes is the reason I created this snack cake in the first place. The surprisingly spicy kick—courtesy of not one, but two kinds of ginger—is tempered by an irresistibly tart, just-sweet-enough lime frosting. So go ahead and cut yourself a square—anytime you want.

½ cup (1 stick) unsalted butter, slightly softened, plus more for greasing

3 cups all-purpose flour

1 tablespoon ground ginger

2 teaspoons ground cinnamon

¼ teaspoon freshly ground black pepper

2 teaspoons baking soda

½ teaspoon fine sea salt

1 cup sugar

2 large eggs

1 cup molasses

1 tablespoon finely minced fresh ginger

1½ cups boiling water

Lime Frosting

Preheat the oven to 300°F. Generously butter a 9 x 13-inch baking pan.

In a medium bowl, whisk together the flour, ground ginger, cinnamon, pepper, baking soda, and salt.

In the bowl of a stand mixer fitted with the paddle attachment, beat the butter and sugar on medium-high speed until light and fluffy, 2 to 3 minutes. Reduce the speed to low and beat in the eggs one at a time until just blended. Add the molasses and fresh ginger and beat until just incorporated. Add the flour mixture in two additions until just combined, beating until blended after each addition. Pour in the boiling water in a slow, steady stream and beat until just blended.

Pour the batter into the prepared pan and bake, turning halfway through for even baking, until a toothpick inserted into the center comes out clean, 45 to 50 minutes. Transfer the pan to a wire rack and cool completely. Frost with lime frosting and cut into 20 equal-size squares.

LIME FROSTING

MAKES 1½ CUPS

1 cup (2 sticks) unsalted butter, slightly softened

2 cups confectioners' sugar, sifted

⅛ teaspoon fine sea salt

1 teaspoon finely grated lime zest

2 tablespoons fresh lime juice

½ teaspoon pure vanilla extract

In the bowl of a stand mixer fitted with the paddle attachment, beat the butter, confectioners' sugar, and salt on medium speed until light and fluffy, 2 to 3 minutes. Add the lime zest and juice and the vanilla and beat until smooth and creamy, 30 seconds.

RHUBARB CORNMEAL UPSIDE-DOWN CAKE

SERVES 8 TO 10

The payoff of an upside-down cake is so great: once you bake, cool, and flip, you get a sweet surprise as the concealed bottom becomes the finished cake's top! In this version, I decided to use rhubarb, one of my favorite seasonal ingredients. Though baking with what is technically a vegetable can be a little intimidating, rhubarb's bright acidic flavor is always a lovely complement as part of a sweet dessert; look for it in early summer when it's at the height of its pucker-inducing power. And while it's true that the cake looks prettier if all the rhubarb is a deep shade of pink, greener stalks of rhubarb will work just fine. This cake's base, with a blend of all-purpose flour and cornmeal, has a toothsome crumb that stands up to the rhubarb's melting softness and sweet-tart flavor.

✱ Tip: Since the unbaked batter can be a bit runny, we recommend wrapping the spring-form pan in aluminum foil for an extra layer of insurance against leaks. Once baked, make sure to follow the directions, letting the cake sit, inverted, in its pan before releasing the outer ring—this will ensure that all the rhubarb ends up on top of your cake—not stuck in the pan.

FOR THE RHUBARB BOTTOM:

1½ pounds fresh rhubarb, trimmed and cut on an angle into 1½-inch pieces (about 4 cups)

½ cup lightly packed light brown sugar

1 tablespoon cornstarch

FOR THE CORNMEAL BATTER:

1¼ cups all-purpose flour

½ cup fine yellow cornmeal or instant polenta

1½ teaspoons baking powder

½ teaspoon baking soda

¼ teaspoon fine sea salt

1 cup sugar

10 tablespoons (1¼ sticks) unsalted butter, slightly softened, plus 4 tablespoons (½ stick)

2 teaspoons pure vanilla extract

1 teaspoon finely grated lemon zest

3 large eggs

¾ cup full-fat sour cream

½ cup lightly packed light brown sugar

Sweet Whipped Cream (page 68)

Line a baking sheet with aluminum foil. Wrap the outside (bottom and sides) of a 10-inch springform pan with aluminum foil and set it on the baking sheet.✱

MAKE THE RHUBARB BOTTOM:

In a large bowl, toss together the rhubarb, brown sugar, and cornstarch.

MAKE THE CORNMEAL BATTER:

In a large bowl, whisk together the flour, cornmeal, baking powder, baking soda, and salt.

In the bowl of a stand mixer fitted with the paddle attachment, beat the sugar with 10 tablespoons of the butter on medium speed until light and fluffy, 2 to 3 minutes. Add the vanilla and lemon zest and beat until just blended. Add the eggs one at a time, beating until fully blended between additions. Reduce the speed to low and add half the flour mixture, then the sour cream, then the remaining flour mixture, beating until just blended after each addition.

Preheat the oven to 325°F.

In a small saucepan melt the remaining 4 tablespoons butter with the brown sugar over medium heat, stirring often, until the mixture is bubbling and the sugar has partially dissolved, 2 minutes. Drizzle the mixture evenly over the bottom of the foil-lined pan, then pour the rhubarb into the pan, completely covering the bottom and piling the rhubarb slightly higher around the outside of the pan than in the center if you can (the rhubarb sinks slightly on the sides). Pour the batter over the rhubarb, smoothing it out to the sides to evenly cover the surface. Bake, turning halfway through, until the surface is golden and a toothpick inserted into the center comes out clean, 65 to 70 minutes. Cool on a wire rack for 15 to 20 minutes, run a sharp knife around the rim of the cake, then invert the cake onto a serving platter and let it sit, still in the springform pan, for 5 minutes. Remove and discard the foil from the outside of the pan, then release and remove the springform ring from the pan. Cool to room temperature and serve with whipped cream.

BLUEBERRY BUCKLE

SERVES 15

Fruit desserts have all sorts of interesting names—crisp, betty, cobbler. For me, it's all about the buckle, which is aptly named for the streusel topping that can cause the top of the cake to sink slightly. I wanted the batter to have all the tenderness of a coffee cake so the crumb would soak up all the deliciousness of the bursting blueberries. My topping, filled with the crunch of toasty pecans and the warmth of cinnamon, makes this a great after-school snack cake—though I love a piece with my morning coffee!

FOR THE PECAN TOPPING:

1 cup all-purpose flour

½ cup (1 stick) cold unsalted butter, cut into pea-size pieces

½ cup lightly packed light brown sugar

½ cup chopped pecans

1 teaspoon ground cinnamon

⅛ teaspoon fine sea salt

FOR THE BUCKLE:

¾ cup (1½ sticks) unsalted butter, slightly softened, plus more

for greasing

3 cups all-purpose flour

1 tablespoon baking powder

½ teaspoon fine sea salt

¾ cup whole milk

2 teaspoons pure vanilla extract

1 cup sugar

2 teaspoons finely grated lemon zest

2 large eggs

3 cups fresh blueberries

MAKE THE PECAN TOPPING:

In a medium bowl, combine the flour, butter, brown sugar, pecans, cinnamon, and salt. Using your fingers, pinch the ingredients together until the mixture is clumpy but still crumbly.

MAKE THE BUCKLE:

Preheat the oven to 350°F. Generously butter a 9 x 13-inch baking pan.

In a medium bowl, combine the flour, baking powder, and salt. In a small bowl stir together the milk and vanilla.

In the bowl of a stand mixer fitted with the paddle attachment, beat the butter, sugar, and lemon zest on medium-high speed until light and fluffy, 2 to 3 minutes. Reduce the speed to low, add the eggs one at a time, and beat until blended. Add half the flour mixture, then the milk mixture, then the remaining flour mixture, beating after each addition until just blended. Using a silicone spatula, gently fold in the blueberries until just incorporated.

Spread the batter evenly into the prepared baking pan, then sprinkle the topping evenly over the cake. Bake until the top is golden brown and a toothpick inserted into the center comes out clean, 40 to 45 minutes. Transfer to a wire rack and cool completely, then cut into 2½ x 3-inch pieces.

BLACK & TAN GUINNESS CAKE

SERVES 12

Guinness cake is well known in England, where its star ingredient—deep, slightly bitter ale—is a pub tradition. A whole bottle of Guinness goes into this batter; that, along with two kinds of chocolate, makes for a tender and flavorful cake. I integrate the beer into all parts of the recipe by making a syrup you brush right onto the cake and whip into a super-creamy frosting. A slice of the finished creation, with its deep-brown bottom and layer of white on top—looks like a freshly poured pint!

FOR THE GUINNESS SYRUP:

½ cup canned or bottled Guinness beer

⅔ cup sugar

FOR THE GUINNESS CAKE:

1 cup (2 sticks) unsalted butter, plus more for greasing

1½ cups canned or bottled Guinness beer

3 ounces dark chocolate (at least 70 percent), finely chopped

3 cups sugar

1 cup unsweetened cocoa powder, sifted

1¼ cups crème fraîche

3 large eggs

2 tablespoons pure vanilla extract

3 cups all-purpose flour

1 tablespoon baking powder

¼ teaspoon fine sea salt

CRÈME FRAÎCHE–GUINNESS FROSTING:

¾ cup (1½ sticks) butter, slightly softened

1½ (8-ounce) packages cream cheese, slightly softened

1 cup confectioners' sugar, sifted

¼ cup Guinness syrup

½ cup crème fraîche

In the bowl of a stand mixer fitted with the paddle attachment, beat the butter and cream cheese on medium-high speed until creamy and slightly fluffy, 2 to 3 minutes. Add the confectioners' sugar and Guinness syrup and beat until smooth, 1 minute. Add the crème fraîche and beat until creamy, 30 seconds more. Frost the cooled cake with the Guinness frosting.

MAKE THE GUINNESS SYRUP:

Slowly pour the Guinness into a small (2-quart) saucepan at an angle (this prevents too much foam) and bring to a very low boil over medium-low heat; skim and discard any foam that gathers on the top. Add the granulated sugar and simmer over very low heat until the mixture thickens slightly and large bubbles form all over the surface, about 10 minutes (you should have about ½ cup syrup). Remove from the heat, transfer to a bowl, and cool to room temperature.

MAKE THE GUINNESS CAKE:

Preheat the oven to 350°F. Butter a 9 x 13-inch baking pan, then line with two strips of parchment paper that fit the pan both vertically and horizontally, leaving a 2-inch overhang on all sides, and generously butter the parchment.

Into a medium saucepan, slowly pour in the Guinness at an angle (this prevents too much foam), add the butter, bring to a low boil over medium-low heat, add the chocolate, and whisk until just melted. Add the sugar and cocoa powder and whisk until the sugar is blended (some sugar granules may remain, and that's okay), 1 minute. Remove from the heat and cool for 10 minutes.

In a large bowl, whisk together the crème fraîche, eggs, and vanilla. Whisk ½ cup of the cooled beer-chocolate mixture into the egg mixture to temper it, then whisk in the rest of the beer mixture until incorporated.

In a medium bowl, whisk together the flour, baking powder, and salt, then add the flour mixture to the chocolate mixture and whisk until smooth.

Pour the mixture into the prepared pan and bake until the outsides of the cake are cracked, the top is dry and slightly hardened, and a toothpick inserted into the center comes out clean, 43 to 45 minutes. Remove the cake from the oven, poke some holes into the cake with a skewer or a chopstick, and brush the cake with ¼ cup of the Guinness syrup while the cake is still warm. Transfer the pan to a wire rack and cool completely. Frost with Crème Fraîche–Guinness Frosting.

PEACH STREUSEL COFFEE CAKE

SERVES 8 TO 10

As a kid, I always looked forward to my mom's special coffee cake, which had a cinnamon streusel topping and a swirl of the same baked into the center so that every bite had a spiced, nutty accent. I thought there was no improving upon the original, so imagine my delight when, on a recent trip to visit my parents, Mom surprised me with this updated version of her old classic. The whole wheat pastry flour and wheat germ add a toastiness that will make you feel a bit more virtuous with every bite.

FOR THE STREUSEL TOPPING:

1 cup chopped walnuts

½ cup sugar

¼ cup whole wheat pastry flour

4 tablespoons (½ stick) unsalted butter, softened

¼ cup lightly packed light brown sugar

2 teaspoons ground cinnamon

⅛ teaspoon fine sea salt

FOR THE FRUIT:

2 large ripe peaches, peeled, pitted, and sliced ½ inch thick, or 2 cups frozen sliced peaches, defrosted

1 tablespoon sugar

½ teaspoon ground cinnamon

½ teaspoon pure vanilla extract

Pinch of fine sea salt

FOR THE CAKE BATTER:

½ cup (1 stick) unsalted butter, slightly softened, plus more for greasing

2 cups whole wheat pastry flour, sifted

1½ teaspoons baking powder

¾ teaspoon baking soda

½ teaspoon fine sea salt

¼ cup toasted wheat germ

1¼ cups sugar

1 cup full-fat sour cream or Greek yogurt

2 large eggs

1½ teaspoons pure vanilla extract

Chilled heavy cream, for serving

MAKE THE STREUSEL TOPPING:

In a medium bowl, combine the walnuts, sugar, flour, butter, brown sugar, cinnamon, and salt. Pinch the mixture together with your fingers to form small clumps.

(Continued)

PREPARE THE FRUIT:

In a medium bowl, gently toss the peaches, sugar, cinnamon, vanilla, and salt.

MAKE THE CAKE BATTER:

Preheat the oven to 350°F. Generously butter a standard-size Bundt pan.

Sift the flour, baking powder, baking soda, and salt into a small bowl and stir in the wheat germ. In the bowl of a stand mixer fitted with the paddle attachment, beat the sugar and butter at high speed until light and creamy, 1 to 2 minutes. Reduce the speed to low, add the sour cream, eggs, and vanilla, return the speed to high and beat until fully blended, 1 to 2 minutes. Lower the speed to medium, gradually add the flour mixture, and beat until just blended, being careful not to overbeat, 1 minute.

ASSEMBLE AND BAKE THE CAKE:

Pour half the batter into the pan, then sprinkle on half the streusel mixture. Top with the peaches, then repeat with the remaining batter and streusel. Bake until the cake is golden and a toothpick inserted into the center comes out clean, 45 to 50 minutes. Cool completely on a wire rack before releasing the cake from the pan. Slice and serve with a pour of heavy cream.

PAMELA SALZMAN'S GRAIN-FREE CINNAMON APPLE CAKE

SERVES 9

Pamela Salzman is a gifted cooking instructor whose classes introduce inspired menus with a whole-foods twist. She is masterful at making good-for-you foods taste amazing, and educates her eager students on how to make the most healthful—and delicious—choices. When Pamela makes a dessert, she eschews refined sugar and white flour, but this apple cake leaves grains out altogether. I was completely amazed upon tasting it for the first time; the base of the cake is made entirely of almond butter, but it tastes just like "regular" cake! I prefer the shredded-apple and pecan version of this magical, mystical treat, but chopped raisins and apples work equally well.

Unrefined coconut oil or unsalted butter, for greasing

1 cup unsweetened smooth almond butter (or sunflower butter for a nut-free cake)

⅓ cup pure maple syrup or raw honey

1 large egg

1 teaspoon pure vanilla extract

1 teaspoon ground cinnamon

¼ teaspoon freshly grated nutmeg

1 teaspoon baking soda

¼ teaspoon fine sea salt

2 medium apples, peeled, cored, and grated (1½ cups)

½ cup chopped pecans (or raisins, for a nut-free cake)

Pamela's Whipped Coconut Cream

Preheat the oven to 350°F. Lightly grease an 8-inch square pan with the coconut oil. Line the pan with two strips of parchment paper that fit the pan both vertically and horizontally, leaving a 2-inch overhang on all sides. Lightly grease the top of the parchment with coconut oil.

In a large bowl, mix the almond butter, maple syrup, egg, vanilla, cinnamon, nutmeg, baking soda, and salt with a wooden spoon until smooth. Fold in the apples and pecans, transfer the batter into the prepared pan, and bake until just set and a toothpick inserted into the center comes out clean or with dry crumbs attached, 40 to 45 minutes, making sure not to overbake. Cool completely in the pan, then cut into nine equal-size pieces. Serve with whipped coconut cream.

PAMELA'S WHIPPED COCONUT CREAM

MAKES 1½ CUPS

1 (14-ounce) can coconut cream* like Trader Joe's brand

½ teaspoon pure vanilla extract

stevia drops to taste

Chill the unopened can of coconut cream in the refrigerator for at least 8 hours and up to 24 hours. Chill the bowl and whisk attachment of a stand mixer for at least 20 minutes. Invert the can and, using a can opener, open the bottom of the can. Pour off any thin liquid; you will be left with a waxy, solidified, shortening-like cream. Remove the mixer bowl and whisk from the freezer, scoop the solidified cream into the bowl, add the vanilla and stevia, and whip on medium-high speed until soft peaks form, 1½ minutes. Serve immediately.

* If you can't find this, you can use full-fat coconut milk.

CHAPTER 11

SPECIAL OCCASION CAKES

Not many people know that my path to Sprinkles began with truly "fancy" cakes: elaborate, multitiered, labor-intensive projects complete with fondant decorations and piped buttercreams. They were my first calling after pastry school because I wanted to make artful creations. But I soon learned that complex "occasion" cakes needed to be made in stages...and that by the time they were delivered, they were not exactly "freshly baked."

I discovered that, for me, the most joyful part of cake making was making simple, delicious, freshly baked cakes that were beautiful but not overly fussy. And that became my new definition of "special occasion." These are cakes that may have additional elements beyond simple cake and frosting, but with simple, easy-to-execute steps and techniques. These freshly baked creations are destined to wow your dinner party guests... and look gorgeous on that cake pedestal.

RICOTTA VANILLA BEAN CHEESECAKE

SERVES 10 TO 12

When I set about developing a cheesecake, I wanted to arrive at a recipe that would please both camps: those who love a light, fluffy variety and people who crave the dense, velvety experience of a New York–style cheesecake. I'm pleased to report that I've created a cake that is light and rich at the same time. The addition of ricotta cheese is the key here; it adds levity without sacrificing richness. And if you've never used a bain-marie (hot-water bath) in your oven before, fear not: this French baking trick helps prevent delicate desserts from drying out and their tops from cracking.

FOR THE GRAHAM CRUST:

8 whole graham crackers (16 squares)

4 tablespoons (½ stick) unsalted butter, melted, plus more for greasing

1 tablespoon sugar

FOR THE RICOTTA–CREAM CHEESE FILLING:

1½ pounds whole-milk ricotta cheese (3 cups)

1 (8-ounce) package cream cheese, slightly softened

1 cup sugar

3 tablespoons all-purpose flour

¼ teaspoon fine sea salt

3 large eggs

2 egg yolks

1 teaspoon freshly grated lemon zest

1 vanilla bean, halved lengthwise and seeds scraped

MAKE THE GRAHAM CRUST:

Preheat the oven to 350°F.

In a food processor, process the graham crackers into fine crumbs (you can also seal them in a zip-top bag, then roll a rolling pin over the bag to make crumbs by hand) and transfer to a medium bowl. Add the butter and sugar and stir until the crumbs are moistened. Press the mixture evenly into the bottom of a 9-inch springform pan and bake until the crust is fragrant and golden, 10 minutes. Cool the pan on a wire rack.

MAKE THE RICOTTA–CREAM CHEESE FILLING:

Line a fine-mesh strainer with a coffee filter or paper towel, place the ricotta on top, and strain for 1 hour to remove excess liquid.

Preheat the oven to 350°F.

In the bowl of a stand mixer fitted with the paddle attachment, beat the drained ricotta, cream cheese, and sugar on medium speed until smooth, 1 to 2 minutes. Reduce the speed to low, add the flour and salt, and beat until incorporated, 1 minute. With the mixer running, add the eggs and egg yolks one at a time and beat until just blended, 1 minute. Stir in the lemon zest and the vanilla bean seeds.

Pour the filling over the cooled graham cracker crust. Set a rimmed baking sheet or large roasting pan in the lower rack of the oven and fill it halfway with boiling water. Arrange a rack above the water bath and bake the cheesecake until just barely set in the center, 1 hour.

Transfer the cheesecake to a wire rack and cool completely. Cover and chill until completely cold, at least 4 hours and preferably overnight. Unmold the cake from the springform pan and transfer to a serving platter.

ANGEL FOOD CAKE WITH ORANGE-VANILLA GLAZE

SERVES 12

Why, oh, why did angel food cake ever disappear? We were all about it (after a brief but intense baklava period) in my house in the eighties, but then it went the way of shoulder pads and leg warmers. Light, airy, and sweet, with a texture completely unto itself, it was the original low-fat dessert that didn't seem like one! I introduced my eight-year-old son to angel food cake this year, and he shocked me by requesting it for his birthday cake—and this was coming from a die-hard Sprinkles loyalist! It's always perfect topped with cream and fruit, but here an orange-scented glaze dresses things up. I made it this way for my son's birthday as promised, adorned (naturally) with a soccer ball candle. Maybe it's time for the Sprinkles angel food cupcake?

FOR THE ANGEL FOOD CAKE:

Distilled white vinegar, for the pan

1 cup cake flour

1½ cups sugar

12 large egg whites, at room temperature

1½ teaspoons cream of tartar

¼ teaspoon fine sea salt

1 teaspoon pure vanilla extract

½ teaspoon almond extract

FOR THE ORANGE–VANILLA GLAZE:

3 tablespoons unsalted butter

1¾ cups confectioners' sugar

3 tablespoons fresh orange juice

½ vanilla bean, split and seeds scraped (see vanilla sugar tip, page 65)

Pinch of fine sea salt

MAKE THE ANGEL FOOD CAKE:

Arrange a rack in the center of the oven and preheat the oven to 350°F. Wipe the inside of an angel food cake pan (see box on page 248) with a vinegar-splashed paper towel to eliminate any grease.

In a medium bowl, sift together the cake flour and ¾ cup of the sugar.

In the bowl of a stand mixer fitted with the whisk attachment, beat the egg whites, cream of tartar, and salt on medium speed until soft peaks form, 3 to 4 minutes. Add the remaining ¾ cup sugar, raise the speed to high, and whip until stiff peaks form and the mixture thickens, 2 to 3 minutes. Reduce the speed to low and slowly add in the flour-sugar mixture, vanilla, and almond extract until just combined. Pour the batter into the pan, using a silicone spatula to evenly spread the batter. Gently tap the pan against the counter to remove any excess air bubbles. Bake until the top is a deep golden brown with slight cracks, springs back when gently pressed, and a toothpick inserted into the center comes out clean, 33 to 34 minutes. Invert the pan onto its "cooling feet," if your pan has them, or by slipping the center cylinder over a glass bottle. Cool completely, upside down, about 2 hours.

MAKE THE ORANGE–VANILLA GLAZE:

In a small saucepan, melt the butter over low heat, then whisk in the confectioners' sugar in two additions until smooth. Add the orange juice, vanilla bean seeds, and salt and whisk until the mixture thickens and coats the back of a spoon, 3 to 4 minutes. Remove from the heat and cool until thickened, 30 minutes.

ASSEMBLE THE CAKE:

Once cool, turn the pan right-side up and remove the cake by lifting up on the center cylinder. (Run a knife or long metal spatula around the edge if the cake needs help releasing.) Finally, invert the cake onto a serving plate and remove the pan.

Drizzle with the glaze.

ANGEL FOOD CAKE PAN

Though you could get away with making this cake in a regular Bundt pan, an angel food cake pan is a worthwhile investment if you'll be making the cake on a regular basis. Tall and straight with a tubular center, angel food cake pans are, by design, made of light materials that encourage maximum air circulation. Look for one *not* made of nonstick materials, which allows the delicate, very airy dough to climb up the sides and rise to the highest heights possible.

STACKED GERMAN CHOCOLATE CAKE

SERVES 8

This is one of those desserts that gets a bad rap. Granted, some people don't love coconut, one of its star ingredients, but I think it's mostly because many varieties of German chocolate cake are cloyingly sweet. I absolutely love this dressed-up version, in which a layer of bittersweet ganache balances the other elements and you can really taste the coconut itself. The stacked linear shape, with naked, unfrosted sides, makes it clean, modern, and new.

FOR THE CAKE:

Butter, for greasing

2 ounces bittersweet chocolate, chopped

2 tablespoons unsweetened cocoa powder

¼ cup boiling water

1¼ cups all-purpose flour

½ teaspoon baking soda

½ teaspoon fine sea salt

½ cup coconut oil

¾ cup sugar

¼ cup lightly packed light brown sugar

2 large eggs, separated

¾ teaspoon pure vanilla extract

½ cup buttermilk, shaken

FOR THE COCONUT PECAN TOPPING:

½ cup heavy cream

1½ teaspoons cornstarch

½ cup sugar

2 egg yolks, lightly whisked

2 tablespoons unsalted butter

½ teaspoon pure vanilla extract

¾ cup finely shredded unsweetened coconut

¾ cup chopped pecans

½ recipe Ganache (page 49), at room temperature

MAKE THE CAKE:

Preheat the oven to 350°F. Butter a 9 x 13-inch baking pan, then line with two strips of parchment paper that fit the pan both vertically and horizontally, leaving a 2-inch overhang on all sides, and generously butter the parchment.

Place the chocolate and cocoa powder in a small heatproof bowl and pour the boiling water over the top; stir until smooth.

In a medium bowl, combine the flour, baking soda, and salt.

In the bowl of a stand mixer fitted with the paddle attachment, beat the coconut oil and sugars on medium-high speed until light and fluffy, 3 to 4 minutes. Beat in the egg yolks one at a time, until just incorporated. Reduce the speed to low and beat in the chocolate mixture and vanilla until just combined. Add half the flour mixture, then the buttermilk, then the remaining flour mixture, beating after each addition until just blended.

In a separate stand mixer bowl and using the whisk attachment, whip the egg whites on high speed until they form stiff peaks, 4 to 5 minutes. Using a silicone spatula, gently fold the egg whites into the batter by hand. Pour the batter into the prepared pan and bake until the cake springs back when gently pressed and a toothpick inserted into the center comes out clean, approximately 25 minutes. Transfer the pan to a wire rack and cool completely.

MAKE THE COCONUT PECAN TOPPING:

In a medium saucepan, combine the cream, cornstarch, sugar, egg yolks, butter, and vanilla. Cook over medium heat, stirring occasionally, until the mixture begins to bubble and thicken, 10 minutes. Cook, stirring, for 2 minutes more, and remove from the heat. Fold in the coconut and pecans until evenly distributed. Cool until thickened, 30 minutes.

BUILD THE CAKE:

Use the parchment paper to lift the cake out of the pan and place it on a flat work surface. Using a serrated knife, slice the cake horizontally into three equal-size rectangles, approximately 4½ x 9 inches each (you are going to stack these layers).

Set aside 2 tablespoons of the ganache. Using an offset spatula, coat the first cake with ¼ cup of the ganache, then cover evenly with 1⅓ cups of the coconut pecan topping. Repeat with the remaining cake layers, ganache, and topping, leaving the sides of the cake "naked." Drizzle with the reserved 2 tablespoons ganache, then let the cake set for 1 to 2 hours before slicing.

SOUR CREAM RUM BUNDT CAKE

SERVES 12 TO 14

Although my family moved around often, my husband, Charles, spent his entire childhood in Oklahoma City. I love his tightly knit community's many long-established traditions, one of which I've been lucky to benefit from every year: the holiday drop-off. Beginning around December 15 all the way through Christmas Eve, the doorbell is on fire, with friends, family, and colleagues popping by with home-baked treats. By the time Charles and I arrive to his parents' house for the holidays, the tins, baskets, and cellophane explosions are piled high—and that bell is still ringing. The array of cookies, toffee, peanut brittle, and fudge is almost mind-boggling, and then there is a rum cake so good I dared to ask for the secret recipe. You can imagine how that request turned out, so I decided to make my own.

This version, with its moist, sour cream–enriched base and boozy topping, is so good it would even pass muster at an Oklahoma holiday drop-off—just be sure to bake an extra to keep around the house for yourself.

FOR THE SOUR CREAM CAKE:

¾ cup (1½ sticks) unsalted butter, slightly softened, plus more for greasing

2 cups sugar, plus more for coating the pan

3 cups cake flour

¾ teaspoon baking soda

½ teaspoon baking powder

½ teaspoon fine sea salt

5 large eggs

1 tablespoon pure vanilla extract

1 cup full-fat sour cream

FOR THE RUM GLAZE AND TOPPING:

½ cup (1 stick) unsalted butter

2 tablespoons whole milk

2 cups confectioners' sugar, sifted

¼ cup dark rum

1 vanilla bean, halved lengthwise and seeds scraped

⅛ teaspoon fine sea salt

1 cup chopped toasted pecans

MAKE THE SOUR CREAM CAKE:

Preheat the oven to 350°F. Butter a 10- to 12-cup Bundt pan, then coat it with granulated sugar and tap out the excess.

In a medium bowl, sift together the flour, baking soda, baking powder, and salt. In a small bowl, lightly whisk the eggs and vanilla.

In the bowl of a stand mixer fitted with the paddle attachment, beat the butter and sugar on medium-high speed until light and fluffy, 2 to 3 minutes. Reduce the speed to low, then slowly add the egg mixture and beat until just blended, 1 minute. Add one-third of the flour mixture and beat until just blended, followed by half the sour cream, then half the remaining flour mixture, the remaining sour cream, and finally the remaining flour mixture, beating until the batter is just smooth and no streaks of flour remain.

Transfer the batter to the prepared pan and bake until the cake springs back when gently pressed and a toothpick inserted into the center comes out clean, 50 to 55 minutes. Transfer to a wire rack and cool for 20 minutes, then invert the cake out of the pan onto the rack and cool completely.

MAKE THE RUM GLAZE AND TOPPING:

In a small saucepan, melt the butter over low heat. Add the milk, then stir in the confectioners' sugar 1 cup at a time until smooth. Add the rum, vanilla bean seeds, and salt and cook, stirring, until slightly thickened, 1 to 2 minutes. Remove from the heat and cool until thickened, 30 minutes.

GLAZE THE CAKE:

Set a baking pan underneath the cooling rack. Using a wooden skewer or chopstick, poke holes all over the surface of the cake. Drizzle half the glaze over the surface of the cake, allowing the excess to drip onto the baking sheet. Sprinkle half the pecans over the glaze, pressing slightly to adhere to the cake if necessary. Drizzle the remaining glaze over the cake (you can also spoon any glaze from the pan back onto the top of the cake), and top with the remaining pecans.

REESE WITHERSPOON'S GRANDMA DRAPER'S SOUR CREAM CAKE WITH PRALINE FROSTING

SERVES 12 TO 14

The world knows Reese Witherspoon as a preternaturally talented Academy Award–winning actress; I am lucky to also know her as a friend, loving mama, and proper Southern girl through and through. You need look no further than her company, Draper James, where the pride she takes in her Nashville upbringing is on display in every monogrammed pillow and magnolia-printed top. Draper James was named after her grandparents, Dorothea Draper and William James, whom Reese credits with teaching her everything she knows about gracious Southern living.

Dorothea would spoil Reese with this stunningly delicious cake. Rich, decadent, and piled two tiers high, it's perfect for a party. The cooked praline icing, sweet and almost sculptable, is ideal for etching feminine swooshes and swirls. As Reese would say, "Y'all, this cake is so good!"

FOR THE SOUR CREAM CAKE:

¾ cup (1½ sticks) unsalted butter, slightly softened, plus more for greasing

3 cups cake flour, plus more for flouring the pans

½ teaspoon baking soda

½ teaspoon baking powder

½ teaspoon fine sea salt

1¼ cups full-fat sour cream

4 teaspoons pure vanilla extract

2 cups sugar

6 large eggs

FOR THE PRALINE FROSTING:

½ cup (1 stick) unsalted butter, slightly softened

½ cup lightly packed dark brown sugar

½ cup heavy cream, plus more if necessary

3¾ cups confectioners' sugar, sifted

1 teaspoon pure vanilla extract

(Continued)

MAKE THE SOUR CREAM CAKE:

Preheat the oven to 325°F. Butter two 9-inch round cake pans, line the bottoms with parchment paper cut to fit, and butter the parchment. Flour the pans, coating the bottom and sides of each pan, then tap out the excess flour.

In a medium bowl, sift together the flour, baking soda, baking powder, and salt. In a small bowl, stir together the sour cream and vanilla.

In the bowl of a stand mixer fitted with the paddle attachment, beat the butter and sugar on medium-high speed until light and smooth, 2 to 3 minutes. Reduce the speed to low, then slowly add the eggs and beat until blended. Stir in one-third of the flour mixture until just blended, followed by half the sour cream mixture, then half the remaining flour mixture, the remaining sour cream mixture, and finally the remaining flour mixture until the batter is smooth and blended and no streaks of flour remain, 2 minutes total.

Transfer the batter to the prepared pans and bake until the cake springs back when gently pressed and a toothpick inserted into the center comes out clean, about 30 minutes. Cool the cakes completely on a wire rack and then invert them onto cake rounds or another flat surface, such as a platter or revolving cake stand.

MAKE THE PRALINE FROSTING:

In a saucepan, melt the butter over medium heat. Stir in the brown sugar and cream, bring to a boil, then immediately pour into the bowl of a stand mixer fitted with the paddle attachment. Add the confectioners' sugar and vanilla, and beat over medium speed until it reaches a spreadable consistency, adding more cream 1 tablespoon at a time if the frosting gets too thick.

Working quickly (the frosting hardens fast!), dollop ¾ cup of the frosting on one cake layer, then stack another layer on top. Still working quickly, frost the top and sides of the cake. Use a knife or offset spatula to create pretty peaks and waves.

VANILLA YULE LOG WITH SUGARED CRANBERRIES

SERVES 8

The first holiday season after I graduated from pastry school, I started a small "business" baking Yule logs, which all my kind and supportive friends bought for their holiday parties. I worked furiously straight through December, painstakingly rolling each sponge cake with a rich layer of buttercream, then covering it with chocolate ganache I'd rake with a fork to make realistic barklike marks before garnishing each creation with cocoa-dusted mushroom meringues. I'm exhausted just thinking about it!

This Yule log, on the other hand, is a cinch to make. The foolproof sponge cake is made extra light and airy thanks to folded-in egg whites and tender cake flour. Combining the cake with a simple whipped cream filling that can be flavored for versatility creates a light, not-too-sweet treat. Dust with confectioners' sugar and cocoa and, if you're feeling fancy, roll some cranberries in sugar for a holiday accent.

FOR THE VANILLA SPONGE CAKE:

2½ tablespoons vegetable oil, plus more for greasing

½ cup cake flour, plus more for flouring the pan

1 tablespoon cornstarch

¼ teaspoon baking powder

3 large eggs, separated

5 tablespoons plus 1 teaspoon sugar

2½ tablespoons vegetable oil

2 tablespoons whole milk

FOR THE SUGARED CRANBERRIES:

1½ cups sugar

½ cup water

1½ cups fresh cranberries

Sweet Whipped Cream (page 68)

Confectioners' sugar, for dusting

Unsweetened cocoa powder, for dusting

MAKE THE VANILLA SPONGE CAKE:

Preheat the oven to 350°F. Lightly oil a straight-sided 9 x 13-inch metal baking pan or quarter sheet pan (9½ x 13 inches), then line the pan with two strips of parchment paper that fit the pan both vertically and horizontally, leaving a 2-inch overhang on all sides. Grease and flour the parchment, then tap out the excess flour.

Dust a clean, lint-free kitchen towel with confectioners' sugar through a fine-mesh sieve. Set aside.

In a small bowl, sift together the flour, cornstarch, and baking powder. In a large bowl, whisk together the egg yolks and 2½ table-spoons of the granulated sugar. Whisk in the oil and the milk until the mixture is light yellow and fully emulsified, 1 minute. Fold in the flour mixture just until there are no lumps.

In the bowl of a stand mixer fitted with the whisk attachment or in a large bowl using a hand mixer, whip the egg whites until soft peaks form, add remaining 2½ tablespoons of the sugar to the egg whites, and whip until stiff peaks form, 3 to 4 minutes. Fold the egg white mixture into the egg yolk mixture in three parts until the batter is light and airy and everything is just thoroughly combined. Pour the batter into the pan and bake until just dry to the touch, about 10 minutes. As soon as the cake comes out of the oven, invert it onto the kitchen towel. Peel off and discard the parchment paper. Beginning at one short end of the towel, roll up the towel and cake together to the opposite end of the towel. Place the rolled cake and towel on a wire rack and cool completely, about 1 hour.

MAKE THE SUGARED CRANBERRIES:

In a medium saucepan, combine ½ cup of the sugar with the water and cook over medium heat, stirring, until sugar has dissolved, 2 to 3 minutes. Pour the mixture into a heatproof bowl. Stir in cranberries and let soak for 2 hours. Using a slotted spoon, transfer the cran-berries to a wire rack and let them dry for at least 1 hour. Place the remaining 1 cup granulated sugar in a large, shallow bowl. Working in batches, roll the cranberries in the sugar until well coated.

FINISH THE CAKE:

Unroll the cooled cake, leaving it on the kitchen towel. Spread the whipped cream evenly on top of the cake to the edges. Reroll the cake, using the towel to lift and guide it into an even, cylindrical shape and using an offset spatula or butter knife to scrape off any cream that escapes. Using a serrated knife, slice off each end to cre-ate sharp, clean edges. Tap the confectioners' sugar and/or cocoa through a fine-mesh sieve onto the rolled log and garnish with the sugared cranberries.

PEANUT BUTTER PRETZEL BANANA CAKE

SERVES 12

Sometimes, you feel like sinking your teeth into a ridiculous indulgence. For just such occasions, I offer you this: thick layers of springy banana cake blanketed with luscious peanut butter–banana frosting, crowned with caramelized pretzels you make yourself on the stovetop.

Crunchy, creamy, sweet, and salty, this cake covers every last craving. Though most of my cakes call for natural-style peanut butter, I felt that the extra-smooth, supermarket-style variety worked better here—you can certainly use natural-style if you choose. Cutting through the pretzels on top can prevent perfect slices, so this may not be the cake to serve when presentation is paramount. Instead, share with good friends. Or, quite frankly, don't share at all . . .

FOR THE BANANA CAKE:

½ cup (1 stick) unsalted butter, melted, plus more for greasing

2 cups all-purpose flour, plus more for flouring the pans

1 teaspoon baking soda

1 teaspoon fine sea salt

½ cup buttermilk, shaken

1 teaspoon pure vanilla extract

½ cup creamy supermarket-style peanut butter, such as Skippy

¾ cup mashed very ripe banana (1½ large bananas)

¾ cup sugar

¾ cup lightly packed light brown sugar

2 large eggs

FOR THE CANDIED PRETZEL TOPPING:

1 cup sugar

4 tablespoons (½ stick) unsalted butter

¼ teaspoon fine sea salt

4 cups mini pretzels, coarsely chopped

FOR THE PEANUT BUTTER–BANANA FROSTING:

½ cup (1 stick) unsalted butter, slightly softened

½ cup creamy supermarket-style peanut butter, such as Skippy

½ cup mashed very ripe banana (1½ medium bananas)

1 teaspoon pure vanilla extract

¼ teaspoon fine sea salt

4⅓ cups confectioners' sugar, sifted

(Continued)

MAKE THE BANANA CAKE:

Preheat the oven to 325°F. Butter three 8-inch round cake pans, line the bottoms with parchment paper cut to fit, and butter the parchment. Flour the pans, coating the bottom and sides of each pan, then tap out the excess flour.

In a medium bowl, whisk together the flour, baking soda, and salt. In a small bowl, stir together the buttermilk and vanilla.

In the bowl of a stand mixer fitted with the paddle attachment, beat the butter, peanut butter, and banana on medium speed until creamy, 2 to 3 minutes. Add the sugars and eggs and beat until just blended. Add half the flour mixture, then the buttermilk mixture, then the remaining flour mixture, beating after each addition until blended. Divide the batter among the prepared pans and bake until the cake springs back when gently pressed and a toothpick inserted into the center comes out clean, approximately 25 minutes. Cool the cakes completely in the pans on a wire rack and then invert them onto cake rounds or another flat surface, like a platter or revolving cake stand.

MAKE THE CANDIED PRETZEL TOPPING:

Line a baking sheet with parchment paper. In a large nonstick skillet, combine the sugar, butter, and salt and cook over medium heat, stirring occasionally, until the butter has melted, 1 minute. Cook, stirring gently, until the sugar has melted and darkened, 4 to 5 minutes. Add the pretzels and gently stir to coat completely. Transfer to the prepared baking sheet and cool completely.

MAKE THE PEANUT BUTTER–BANANA FROSTING:

In the bowl of a stand mixer fitted with the paddle attachment, beat the butter and peanut butter together until light and fluffy, 1 to 2 minutes. Add the banana, vanilla, and salt and beat until just combined. Slowly add the confectioners' sugar and beat until completely incorporated and creamy, 1 minute.

FROST THE CAKE:

Using a long serrated knife, trim off any uneven or domed parts from the top of each cake to create a flat surface. Place one of the cakes on a serving platter, leveled-side up. Using an offset spatula, frost the top of that layer, then stack another cake layer on top, leveled part facing down, and frost the top of that layer. Stack the third layer on top and create a crumb coat (see page 242). Place the remaining frosting on the top of the cake and, working from the center outward, frost the top and the sides of the cake. Mound the candied pretzels on top of the cake, or press the pretzels onto the sides and top of the cake.

CHAPTER 12

BIRTHDAY CAKES

I remember a birthday cake my mom made for me when I was a little girl, featuring a beautiful Barbie sticking out of a giant ball gown of cake with light blue frosting "ruffles." It was the most incredible thing I had ever seen! These days my cakes may not be quite so fanciful, but for birthdays I still appreciate the magic of a tall layered cake glowing with candles. In this chapter you will find some traditional—and some less expected—ways to make those birthday celebrations extra special. Needless to say, no one has to know whether it's your *actual* birthday—by making one of these fantastic desserts, any day becomes one worthy of celebration.

MRS. FIELDS–INSPIRED CHOCOLATE CHIP COOKIE CAKES

MAKES 2 CAKES (EACH CAKE SERVES 8)

When *Vanity Fair* magazine compared me to Debbi Fields—also known as Mrs. Fields—in her heyday, it felt like the realization of a lifelong dream. It would be accurate to say that Debbi Fields was my childhood idol. I can still remember experiencing her cookies for the very first time, marveling at the novelty of watching them get weighed on the spot to determine the price! Fresh and chewy, studded with chocolate in every bite, they were *so* good I couldn't wait to get to the mall to pick out my cookie. The fact that there was a woman behind this incredible concept only made me extra smitten—and clearly bitten by the desire to emulate my hero.

This recipe is an homage to the famous Mrs. Fields cookie cake, a fun departure from more traditional cakes or cupcakes. It makes two cookie rounds, more than enough to feed a crowd. But if your gathering is more intimate, save one for later; they freeze beautifully.*

* To freeze the second cake, wrap the cooled cake in a layer of plastic wrap followed by a layer of aluminum foil. Freeze for up to 3 months.

1 cup (2 sticks) unsalted butter, slightly softened, plus more for greasing

2¼ cups all-purpose flour, sifted

1 teaspoon baking soda

1 teaspoon fine sea salt

1 cup lightly packed dark brown sugar

⅓ cup sugar

1 large egg

1 egg yolk

1 tablespoon pure vanilla extract

1½ cups semisweet chocolate chips

Ice cream for serving (optional)

Preheat the oven to 350°F. Butter two 9-inch round cake pans.

In a medium bowl, whisk together the flour, baking soda, and salt.

In the bowl of a stand mixer fitted with the paddle attachment, beat the butter and both sugars on medium-high speed until creamy, 2 to 3 minutes. Reduce the speed to low, add the egg, egg yolk, and vanilla, and beat until blended. Add the flour mixture in two parts, beating until blended after each addition. Using a silicone spatula or wooden spoon, fold in the chocolate chips.

Divide the dough between the prepared pans, pressing it down to evenly cover the surface of the pans. Bake until golden and fragrant, 20 minutes. Cool the cookie cakes completely in the pans on a wire rack and then invert them onto a serving platter. Cut into wedges.

Serve with ice cream, if desired.

VEGAN CARROT BIRTHDAY CAKE

SERVES 12 TO 14

File this one under "happens to be vegan"—it's not what's missing that you'll remember, but what's there in spades: big flavor. Ground flaxseed, which often stands in for eggs in vegan dessert recipes, helps give the cake a lift, and vegetable oil—not to mention a whole pound of grated carrots—makes it super moist and tender. There's something about the simplicity of a sheet cake—here frosted with a vegan version of our irresistible cream cheese frosting—that makes every celebration just a little bit sweeter.

1 cup vegetable oil, plus more for greasing

2¼ cups whole wheat pastry flour

1½ teaspoons ground cinnamon

¾ teaspoon freshly grated nutmeg

¼ teaspoon ground ginger

⅛ teaspoon ground cloves

2 teaspoons baking powder

1 teaspoon baking soda

1 teaspoon fine sea salt

¼ cup ground flaxseed

1 cup sugar

½ cup lightly packed light brown sugar

1 pound carrots, scrubbed, trimmed, and grated on large holes of a box grater (3¼ cups)

¾ cup chopped toasted walnuts

½ cup golden raisins

Vegan Cream Cheese Frosting (page 42)

Preheat the oven to 350°F. Grease a 9 x 13-inch baking pan, then line with two strips of parchment paper that fit the pan both vertically and horizontally, leaving a 2-inch overhang on all sides, and generously grease the parchment.

In a medium bowl, whisk together the flour, cinnamon, nutmeg, ginger, cloves, baking powder, baking soda, and salt. In the bowl of a stand mixer fitted with the paddle attachment, combine the ground flaxseed and ¾ cup water, then add the sugars and beat for 1 minute. With the mixer running, add the oil in a slow stream and beat until blended. Slowly add the flour mixture, beating until blended. Using a spatula, stir in the carrots, walnuts, and raisins until incorporated.

Pour the batter into the prepared pan and bake until it springs back when touched and a toothpick inserted into the center comes out clean, 40 to 45 minutes. Cool the cake completely in the pan on a wire rack and frost with vegan cream cheese frosting. Cut into squares to serve.

YELLOW BIRTHDAY CAKE WITH TANGY CHOCOLATE FROSTING

SERVES 12

I am clearly devoted to cupcakes, but on special occasions like an intimate dinner party, I still love a classic layer cake. There's just something about the spectacle of bringing a cake to the table on a gorgeous stand, then slicing into it ceremoniously in front of my guests, that confirms how special a dessert can be. This cake, with fluffy layers and tangy, rich, almost shiny sour cream frosting, is one that a child will love but that an adult will appreciate even more. Top it simply with a single candle or load it with a sea of tall, thin tapers for extra wow factor.

---

1 cup (2 sticks) unsalted butter, slightly softened, plus more for greasing

2 cups cake flour, plus more for flouring the pan

1½ teaspoons baking powder

½ teaspoon baking soda

1 teaspoon fine sea salt

¾ cup buttermilk, shaken

1 tablespoon pure vanilla extract

2 cups sugar

3 large eggs, separated

Tangy Chocolate Frosting

Preheat the oven to 350°F. Butter two 9-inch round cake pans, line the bottoms with parchment paper cut to fit, and butter the parchment. Flour the pans, coating the bottom and sides of each pan, then tap out the excess flour.

In a large bowl, sift together the flour, baking powder, baking soda, and salt. In a glass measuring cup, stir together the buttermilk and vanilla.

In the bowl of a stand mixer fitted with the paddle attachment, beat the butter and sugar until light and fluffy, 2 to 3 minutes. Add the egg yolks and beat until blended. Add half the flour mixture, then the buttermilk mixture, then the remaining flour mixture, beating until blended after each addition.

In a separate stand mixer bowl using the whisk attachment, whip the egg whites until soft peaks form, 1 to 2 minutes. Using a silicone spatula, gently fold the egg whites into the batter until just blended.

Divide the batter evenly between the prepared pans and bake until the cake springs back when lightly touched and a toothpick inserted into the center comes out clean, 30 to 35 minutes. Cool the

TANGY CHOCOLATE FROSTING

1 pound 2 ounces bittersweet chocolate, chopped

4 cups confectioners' sugar

½ cup unsweetened cocoa powder

¼ teaspoon fine sea salt

1½ (8-ounce) packages cream cheese, slightly softened

¾ cup (1½ sticks) unsalted butter, at room temperature

1½ cups sour cream

In a microwave-safe bowl, microwave the chocolate on high for 2 to 3 minutes, stopping and stirring every 45 seconds until melted. Let the chocolate cool to room temperature for 20 to 30 minutes.

In a medium bowl, sift together the confectioners' sugar, cocoa powder, and salt.

In the bowl of a stand mixer fitted with the paddle attachment, beat the cream cheese and butter on medium-high speed until pale and fluffy, 2 minutes. Reduce the speed to low and add the sugar mixture in two parts, followed by the chocolate and the sour cream, beating until blended after each addition and making sure not to incorporate too much air into the frosting.

cakes completely in the pans on a wire rack and then invert them onto cake rounds or another flat surface, like a platter or revolving cake stand.

Using a long serrated knife, trim off any uneven or domed parts from the top of each cake to create a flat surface. Place one of the cakes on a serving platter, leveled-side up. Using an offset spatula, frost the top of that layer, then stack the other cake layer on top, leveled part facing down. Create a crumb coat (see page 242) and place the remaining frosting on the top of the cake. Working from the center outward, frost the top and sides of the cake.

THE SPRINKLES SPRINKLE CAKE

SERVES 8 TO 10

For the ten-year anniversary of the first Sprinkles store, I wanted to launch a new celebratory flavor. I knew it had to be something that would rival our red velvet in terms of popularity—but be unlike anything we had ever done before. Though my brainstorming took me in a million directions, I finally landed on something that had seemingly been right in front of me all along . . . that's right, sprinkles! Ironically, a sprinkle-filled and topped cupcake was something we'd never done, and I knew it was the perfect thing. Also known as Funfetti, this style of cake adornment is alive with color and just begs to be served at a party. For extra wow factor, I've adapted it into a full-size cake. If Sprinkles celebrated its big birthday with one, I know it will be perfect for yours.

½ cup (1 stick) unsalted butter, slightly softened, plus more for greasing

1½ cups all-purpose flour, plus more for flouring the pans

1 teaspoon baking powder

¼ teaspoon baking soda

¼ teaspoon fine sea salt

⅔ cup whole milk

1½ teaspoons pure vanilla extract

1 cup sugar

1 large egg

2 large egg whites

⅓ cup rainbow jimmies-style sprinkles*

Sprinkle Frosting

1 cup sprinkles, either rainbow jimmies-style or nonpareils-style

Preheat the oven to 325°F. Butter two 8-inch round cake pans, line the bottoms with parchment paper cut to fit, and butter the parchment. Flour the pans, coating the bottom and sides of each pan, then tap out the excess flour.

In a medium bowl, whisk together the flour, baking powder, baking soda, and salt. In a small bowl, stir together the milk and vanilla.

In the bowl of a stand mixer fitted with the paddle attachment, beat the butter and sugar on medium-high speed until light and fluffy, 2 to 3 minutes. Reduce the speed to low, add the eggs and egg whites one at a time, and beat until creamy, 1 to 2 minutes. Add half the flour mixture, then the milk mixture, then the remaining flour mixture, beating until blended after each addition. Using a silicone spatula or wooden spoon, gently fold in the ⅓ cup rainbow sprinkles by hand.

SPRINKLE FROSTING

MAKES 2 CUPS

3 cups confectioners' sugar, sifted

1 cup (2 sticks) unsalted butter, slightly softened

⅛ teaspoon fine sea salt

5 teaspoons whole milk

1 teaspoon pure vanilla extract

In the bowl of a stand mixer fitted with the paddle attachment, beat the confectioners' sugar, butter, and salt, starting on low speed and increasing to medium speed, until thick and uniform, 2 to 3 minutes. Add the milk and vanilla and beat until creamy, being careful not to incorporate too much air into the frosting.

Divide the batter evenly between the prepared cake pans and bake until the tops are just dry to the touch and a toothpick inserted into the center comes out clean, 18 to 20 minutes. Transfer the cakes in the pans to a wire rack and cool completely, then invert them onto cake rounds or another flat surface, like a platter or revolving cake stand.

Using a long serrated knife, trim off any uneven or domed parts from the top of each cake layer to create a flat surface. Place one of the cakes on a serving platter, leveled-side up. Using an offset spatula, frost the top of that layer, then stack the other cake layer on top, leveled part facing down. Place the remaining frosting on the top of the cake and, working from the center outward, frost the top and sides of the cake. Place a baking sheet under the serving platter.

Sprinkle the cake all over with the 1 cup sprinkles, catching the fallen sprinkles on the baking sheet.

* **A Note About Sprinkles:**
Though I try to stick to all-natural products, sometimes nothing but the classics will do. That's the case with the sprinkles I use in this visually amazing cake. After a lot of testing, I landed on good old-fashioned primary-colored "jimmies"-style sprinkles; tiny, round nonpareils tend to bleed more into the baked batter (though they can be used to top the frosting). So stick with primary-colored jimmies for the brightest, most festive cake!

NEAPOLITAN ICE CREAM CAKE

SERVES 8 TO 10

I have a special spot in my heart for anything Neapolitan. The combination of chocolate, vanilla, and strawberry is a match made in heaven, and looking at the pink, white, and brown layers stacked in a row instantly transports me to a place of sweet childhood nostalgia. Here I use both cake and ice cream to transform Neapolitan flavors into a celebratory dessert. Once frozen, most cakes become too hard to eat, but I solved that problem by baking a thin layer of airy sponge, yielding cake that can be sliced right out of the freezer. Layered with strawberry ice cream and chewy hot fudge, every slice delivers a beautiful, old-fashioned Neapolitan look with all the best elements of an ice cream sundae!

FOR THE CAKE LAYER AND ICE CREAM:

2½ tablespoons vegetable oil, plus more for oiling the pan

½ cup cake flour, plus more for flouring the pan

1 tablespoon cornstarch

¼ teaspoon baking powder

3 large eggs, separated

5 tablespoons sugar, divided, plus 1 teaspoon

2 tablespoons whole milk

4½ to 5 cups strawberry ice cream, softened

FOR THE HOT FUDGE SAUCE:

⅔ cup heavy cream

2 tablespoons sugar

2 tablespoons lightly packed light brown sugar

1½ teaspoons light corn syrup

4 ounces milk chocolate or milk chocolate chips

1 tablespoon unsalted butter

½ teaspoon fine sea salt

1 teaspoon pure vanilla extract

MAKE THE CAKE:

Preheat the oven to 350°F. Cut a piece of parchment paper to fit the bottom of a 9-inch springform pan. Grease the bottom and sides of the pan, line it with the parchment paper, grease the parchment, and set aside.

In a bowl, sift together the cake flour, cornstarch, and baking powder. In a large bowl, whisk together the egg yolks and 2½ tablespoons of the sugar. Whisk in the oil and the milk until the mixture is light yellow and fully emulsified, 1 minute. Fold in the sifted dry ingredients just until there are no lumps.

In the bowl of a stand mixer fitted with the whisk attachment or using an electric hand mixer, whip the egg whites until soft peaks form. Add another 2½ tablespoons of sugar to the egg whites and whip until stiff peaks form, 3-4 minutes. Fold the egg white mixture into the egg yolk mixture in three parts until the batter is light and airy and everything is just thoroughly combined.

Pour the batter into the prepared pan and bake until the top is just dry, the cake is springy, and a toothpick inserted into the center comes out clean, 9-10 minutes. Cool the cake completely on a wire rack.

MAKE THE FUDGE:

In a medium saucepan, whisk the cream, both sugars, corn syrup, chocolate, and butter over medium heat until the mixture comes to a boil. Cook, whisking constantly, until the mixture thickens and feels like fudge sauce, 5 minutes. Remove from the heat and whisk in the salt and vanilla. Pour the fudge into a shallow glass dish or bowl to cool. (The fudge pours best when it's not too hot and not too cold, at the consistency of honey; fudge can be made ahead and reheated in a water bath of lukewarm water to the desired consistency.)

ASSEMBLE THE CAKE:

Press the ice cream into the pan on top of the cake, smoothing it with an offset spatula. Freeze the ice cream for 2 hours.

Pour the soft fudge on top of the cake, using an offset spatula sparingly to distribute the fudge evenly. Once the fudge hardens, cover the cake with plastic wrap and freeze the cake for at least one hour and up to 24 hours. To serve, release the side of the springform pan.

Let the cake sit on the counter for 10 minutes for easier slicing. To slice, submerge a large knife in hot water, then quickly wipe to dry and use to slice; rewarm and dry knife as necessary.

CHAPTER 13

CANDIES, PUDDINGS & OTHER SWEETS

If you're looking for an amazing dessert—but also something a little different—you've come to the right place. From strawberry shortcake and sea salt caramels to meringues and mousses, this chapter is a reminder that desserts come in all shapes, sizes, and flavors. Let your mood—and the occasion—inspire you to explore the many possibilities here.

COPPER POT FUDGE

MAKES EIGHTY 1-INCH SQUARES

This recipe transports me to the Cape Cod summers of my teen years, where I had my first real summer job working the register at a fudge and gift shop in Chatham, Massachusetts. I'd arrive early every morning, bleary-eyed, but the smell of fudge being stirred in a giant copper pot in the back of the store always perked me right up. I've updated this classic by removing the corn syrup you find in many recipes; mine allows you to focus on the simple pleasure of fudge so rich, chocolaty, and chewy that you'll find it hard to stop after one square. Copper pot optional!

1 (14-ounce) can sweetened condensed milk

12 ounces semisweet chocolate, finely chopped

6 ounces milk chocolate, finely chopped

⅛ teaspoon fine sea salt

1½ teaspoons pure vanilla extract

Line the bottom and sides of a 9-inch square baking pan with two strips of parchment paper that fit the pan both vertically and horizontally, leaving a 2-inch overhang on all sides. Combine the condensed milk, chocolates, and salt in a heavy-bottomed saucepan. Cook over low heat, stirring, until the chocolate has melted and the mixture becomes thick and shiny, 6 to 7 minutes. Remove from the heat and whisk in the vanilla. Pour the mixture into the prepared pan, smoothing it into the corners with a knife or offset spatula. After a few minutes, take a sharp knife and gently score the fudge into 1-inch pieces. (This will make it easier to cut once it has set.) Let the fudge set at room temperature or in the fridge for at least one hour. Remove the fudge from the pan and cut it into pieces along the scored lines.

CHOCOLATE HAZELNUT MOUSSE

SERVES 6

Nutella, the addictive chocolate-hazelnut spread, is having a moment. The toastiness of the nuts and the undeniable appeal of chocolate makes an unbeatable combination. I suspected that this dynamic duo would work well in a mousse, and I'm happy to report that my "research" yielded fantastic results. I boosted the hazelnut quotient with the addition of hazelnut liqueur, then used little more than good-quality chocolate, milk, and whipped cream to bring it together.

---

6 ounces semisweet chocolate, chopped

¼ cup whole milk

¼ teaspoon fine sea salt

½ cup chocolate-hazelnut spread, such as Nutella

2 tablespoons hazelnut-flavored liqueur, such as Frangelico

1 tablespoon strong prepared coffee, at room temperature

¼ teaspoon pure vanilla extract

1 cup heavy cream

6 Mocha Chip Meringues (page 135), crushed, for garnish

In a small saucepan, combine the chocolate and milk and cook over medium heat, stirring, until melted. Remove from the heat, transfer to a medium bowl, and whisk in the salt, chocolate-hazelnut spread, hazelnut liqueur, coffee, and vanilla until smooth.

In the bowl of a stand mixer fitted with the whisk attachment, or in a medium bowl using a whisk, whip the cream until stiff peaks form, 3 minutes. Using a silicone spatula, gently fold half the cream into the chocolate mixture until just incorporated.

Divide the mixture evenly among six individual dessert glasses, cover each glass with plastic wrap, and chill until set, at least 3 hours and up to 24. Serve topped with the remaining whipped cream and crushed meringues.

RUTH'S PEANUT BRITTLE

SERVES 10 TO 12

Ruth Gorkuscha is a close family friend of my in-laws, the Nelsons, and a masterful candy maker. One of the holiday treats I most look forward to every year is a cheery tin of her famous peanut brittle—the crispest, most delicate and addictive brittle I have ever eaten. I have always raved to her about it, so one year she surprised me by enclosing a notecard with the recipe, originally attributed to her friend Mary Ann. Thank you, Ruth and Mary Ann, for sharing your incredible recipe with me . . . and the world!

Keep in mind that it's not as easy to find raw peanuts as roasted, but I assure you the search is worth it. You can add them earlier in the cooking process, infusing the delicious candy base with extra-deep peanutty flavor. Word to the wise: Be sure to keep stirring those peanuts off the bottom of the saucepan during the last few minutes of cooking to avoid burning them. But even if a couple burn, Ruth assures me, you can always just break that piece off and throw it away. "Pulling" the brittle at the end makes it extra shatteringly thin and, well . . . brittle!

½ cup (1 stick) unsalted butter, plus more for greasing

1 cup light corn syrup

2 cups sugar

2 cups raw unsalted peanuts

½ teaspoon fine sea salt

2 teaspoons baking soda

Butter a large, unrimmed baking sheet or use a Silpat, then butter the counter 10 to 12 inches beyond each side of the sheet to allow for the sticky candy to be stretched off the sides.

In a heavy 4-quart saucepan, combine the corn syrup, sugar, 4 tablespoons of the butter, and ½ cup water. Cook over medium heat, stirring occasionally, until the sugar has dissolved, then raise the heat to medium-high and clip a candy thermometer to the side of the pan. Cook until the mixture reaches 240°F, also known as soft-ball stage.

Add the peanuts, stir well, and cook over medium-high heat, stirring occasionally to keep the peanuts from sticking to the bottom of the pan and burning, until the mixture reaches 300°F, or hard-crack stage, reducing the heat under the pan as the mixture approaches 300°F to ensure it doesn't burn.

At 300°F, quickly take the pan off the heat and add the remaining 4 tablespoons butter and the salt, then add the baking soda and stir continuously as the mixture foams and bubbles. Stir just until the mixture foams uniformly, then pour it onto the prepared baking sheet, spreading it immediately with a silicone spatula. Start to pull with two greased forks while still hot, then, after 4 to 5 minutes, once the mixture has cooled, start pulling with your hands. Do not worry about making holes in the mixture. Stretch the pieces as thin as possible (the brittle will go past the edges of the sheet), and cool completely. Break into uneven shards and enjoy!

✳ Tip: I love using a giant Silpat for pouring the hot liquid, and I smooth and pull as much as I can for that exquisitely fine candy!

CLASSIC STRAWBERRY SHORTCAKES

SERVES 6

I challenge you to find someone who doesn't love strawberry short-cake. It's an almost universal favorite, and for good reason: the combination of a light, flaky base; juicy berries; and a cloud of sweet cream is sheer dessert heaven…not to mention a real crowd-pleaser! At the heart of every great shortcake is a foolproof pastry recipe, and this one gets a lift from a generous helping of baking soda and a tiny bit of crunch, thanks to a sprinkling of turbinado sugar.

Letting the fruit macerate in sugar for a few minutes brings out every drop of juice. I also make the cream topping extra special by folding in crème fraîche and honey; it's subtle, but it takes this dessert to new heights.

FOR THE STRAWBERRIES:

1 pound ripe strawberries, hulled, rinsed, dried, and sliced (3 cups sliced)

¼ cup sugar

Zest of 1 lemon

FOR THE SHORTCAKES:

2 cups all-purpose flour, plus more for dusting

4 teaspoons baking powder

3 tablespoons sugar

⅛ teaspoon fine sea salt

½ cup (1 stick) cold butter, cut into small cubes and refrigerated until ready to use

⅔ cup half-and-half, plus more as needed

2 tablespoons heavy cream

1 tablespoon sanding sugar or turbinado sugar, such as Sugar In The Raw

FOR THE WHIPPED CREAM:

1¼ cups heavy cream

1 teaspoon pure vanilla extract

⅔ cup crème fraîche

3 tablespoons honey

PREPARE THE STRAWBERRIES:

Toss the strawberries, sugar, and lemon zest in a bowl, adding 1 additional tablespoon of sugar if you prefer a sweeter end result. Let the fruit sit for a bit to release some of its juices; chill until ready to use.

MAKE THE SHORTCAKES:

Preheat the oven to 425°F.

In a food processor, pulse the flour, baking powder, sugar, and salt until incorporated, about 5 pulses. Add the butter and pulse until incorporated but with lots of pea-size pieces, 10 to 15 pulses (make sure not to overprocess). Transfer the mixture to a large bowl and stir in the half-and-half until just incorporated and fully moist (do not overwork!), adding more half-and-half a tiny bit at a time, if necessary; the dough will be slightly sticky.

Transfer to a floured work surface and, using floured hands, gently knead twice, then form into a 6 x 1-inch square, adding more flour if necessary. Using a very sharp knife or a pastry cutter, cut the dough in half, then cut across each half two times to create six rectangular shortcakes.* Brush the tops with the cream and sprinkle with the sanding sugar. Bake until the tops are lightly golden and bottoms are slightly deeper golden, 12 to 13 minutes.

MAKE THE WHIPPED CREAM:

While the biscuits are cooling, in the bowl of a stand mixer fitted with the whisk attachment, beat the cream and vanilla on medium-high speed until soft peaks form, 2 to 3 minutes. Add the crème fraîche and honey and beat until incorporated, 30 seconds. Chill until ready to use.

ASSEMBLE THE SHORTCAKES:

Using your hands or a serrated knife, split the shortcakes horizontally and spoon ½ cup of the strawberries and some of the juices onto the open shortcakes. Top each with ½ cup of the whipped cream, then close with the other shortcake half.

✳ **Tip:** When you cut the shortcake dough, try to do it in one swift, strong motion—sawing away at the dough seals the edges, preventing them from lifting to their full potential.

SWEET & SPICY PRALINES

MAKES 30 PRALINES

Though pralines started out in Europe as a chocolate-based dessert with a creamy, nutty filling, Americans—especially Southerners—know them as a buttery pecan treat. I've loved them my whole life (as has my decidedly Southern husband), but I wanted to achieve something a little more grown-up here. By adding cayenne and freshly ground black pepper, the sweetness is tempered by a subtle, but discernible, heat. Of course you can eat them straight, but they're also divine crumbled over a bowl of vanilla ice cream.

1 cup lightly packed light brown sugar

½ cup sugar

½ cup heavy cream

4 tablespoons (½ stick) unsalted butter

1 teaspoon pure vanilla extract

½ teaspoon fine sea salt

¼ teaspoon cayenne pepper

⅛ teaspoon freshly ground black pepper, plus more for sprinkling

2 cups raw, unsalted pecan halves

Flaky sea salt, such as Maldon, for sprinkling

Line a large baking sheet with parchment paper.

In a heavy-bottomed saucepan, combine the sugars, cream, butter, vanilla, fine sea salt, cayenne, black pepper, and 2 tablespoons water and cook over medium-high heat, stirring continuously with a wooden spoon, until the mixture thickens and begins bubbling, 9 to 10 minutes. Turn off the heat, add the pecans, and cook, stirring, until the mixture thickens and loses its shine, 1 minute.

Quickly drop the mixture, 1 tablespoonful at a time, onto the prepared baking sheet, spacing each spoonful 2 inches apart. Immediately sprinkle with the flaky salt and black pepper to taste and cool until firm, 10 to 15 minutes.

PINK PAVLOVA

SERVES 8 TO 10

In Southeast Asia, where I spent part of my childhood, I had lots of friends from Australia and New Zealand, so pavlova—named for a famous Russian ballerina whose visit Down Under caused quite a stir—was a frequent treat. Though Aussies and Kiwis disagree on which country actually invented pavlova, we can all agree it is an incredible creation. The mix of crisp meringue with a marshmallow center, light cream, and sweet, juicy fruit ranks it high on my list of perfect desserts. I have often made pavlovas for dinner parties, and feel almost guilty eliciting so many *oohs* and *aaahs* from my guests, because it's just so simple.

In this recipe, the pavlova is topped with perky red raspberries; I have played with the color and flavor of the whipped cream and meringue to achieve a beautifully shaded ombré effect. Light, fresh, and elegant, it's great for a shower, tea, or lunch with the girls. Don't worry if the slices are less than perfect—they're supposed to be that way!

FOR THE PAVLOVA:

1 teaspoon distilled white vinegar, plus more for wiping the mixer bowl

1 cup superfine sugar

2 teaspoons cornstarch

4 large egg whites, at room temperature

½ teaspoon pure vanilla extract

FOR THE CREAM AND TOPPING:

3¾ cups (about 9 ounces) fresh raspberries, divided

3 tablespoons sugar

1½ cups heavy cream

MAKE THE PAVLOVA:

Preheat the oven to 275°F. Line a large baking sheet with parchment paper, trace a 9-inch circle in dark-colored pen onto the parchment, and flip the parchment over. Dampen a paper towel with vinegar and wipe the inside of a stand mixer bowl to remove any excess oil, then dry with a clean paper towel.

In a small bowl, whisk together the superfine sugar and cornstarch to blend and remove lumps.

In the clean bowl of the stand mixer fitted with the whisk attachment, whip the egg whites on medium speed until foamy. Raise the speed to medium-high and begin adding the sugar-cornstarch mixture 1 tablespoon at a time, until all the sugar has dissolved, 1 minute more. Add the vinegar and beat until the meringue is glossy and holds stiff peaks, approximately 10 minutes more. Using a silicone spatula, fold in the vanilla until incorporated, being careful not to deflate the whipped egg whites.

Scoop the egg white mixture into the circle you drew on the parchment paper, pushing out the sides to form a slight well in the center (to hold the cream and fruit after baking). Bake until the meringue has puffed up and cracked on the top, approximately 1 hour and 15 minutes. Turn off the oven and, with the door closed, let the pavlova cool completely in the oven.

MAKE THE CREAM:

In a blender or food processor, puree 2¼ cups of the raspberries and the sugar until smooth, 30 seconds; press the puree through a fine-mesh sieve into a bowl, using a silicone spatula to force through all the puree; discard the seeds. Either by hand, in the bowl of a stand mixer fitted with the whisk attachment, or with a hand mixer, beat the cream until it forms soft peaks. Gently fold the raspberry puree into the cream.

ASSEMBLE THE PAVLOVA:

Gently peel the pavlova from the parchment paper and set it on a serving platter. Spoon the cream into the center of the pavlova, spreading it outward but leaving a 3-inch meringue border on the edges. Top with the remaining 1½ cups raspberries. Cut into wedges to serve.

JESSICA ALBA'S "I'M IN LOVE WITH THE COCO"

SERVES 6

Known originally as a superstar of screens big and small, Jessica Alba is now equally famous as a passionate mother, lover of all things home, and founder of the incredibly successful Honest Company. Jessica is truly a beauty from the inside out, and her company reflects her own personal values of social responsibility and philanthropy. In 2015, I was fortunate enough to collaborate with her on a charitable cupcake we called Swirl by Jessica Alba. The proceeds went to a cause that she and I both support, Baby2Baby, which provides supplies to needy families with newborns and young children.

Jessica approaches food in the same way she does her lifestyle—by using simple, pure ingredients. The deeply decadent and elegant dessert she graciously shares here also happens to be both dairy- and gluten-free; Jessica recommends using all organic ingredients just like she does. Dense, moist chocolate cake lies beneath a fudgy chocolate-almond coating dusted with confectioners' sugar and sliced toasted almonds. Like Jessica herself, it's beautiful and pure.

* Almond flour can be purchased at health food stores (make sure to buy almond flour, not almond meal, which is ground from un-blanched almonds and therefore not as fine).

Or to make your own almond flour, process raw blanched and skinless almonds in a food processor until fine (but make sure not to overprocess, which will create almond butter!).

ALL INGREDIENTS ORGANIC:

Cooking spray

¾ cup plus ⅓ cup canned full-fat coconut milk (shake the can before opening to incorporate the milk solids)

1½ cups semisweet dairy-free chocolate chips, such as Chocolate Dream

2 teaspoons pure vanilla extract

¼ cup finely ground almond meal or almond flour*

6 large eggs

½ cup cane sugar

1 (7-ounce) package gluten-free almond paste

½ cup sliced almonds, lightly toasted

Confectioners' sugar, for dusting

Preheat the oven to 400°F. Coat six 6-ounce ramekins with cooking spray.

In a small saucepan, heat ¾ cup of the coconut milk over medium heat until bubbling. Add 1 cup of the chocolate chips and cook, stirring, until the chocolate has melted and the mixture is smooth, 2 to 3 minutes. Remove from the heat, whisk in the vanilla, and transfer to a large bowl. Stir in the almond meal until blended.

In the bowl of a stand mixer fitted with the paddle attachment, beat the eggs and cane sugar until creamy, 2 minutes. Gently whisk the egg mixture into the chocolate mixture until well combined.

Divide the batter among the greased ramekins and bake until a toothpick inserted into the center comes out mostly clean, 24 to 25 minutes. Cool for 1 hour, then refrigerate, uncovered, until set, 1 hour more.

Remove the cakes from the refrigerator and let them come to room temperature, 30 minutes. Condense the cakes by pressing down on each one gently with the back of a spoon.

On a clean work surface, roll out the almond paste to about ⅛-inch thickness. Using a 3½-inch round cookie cutter or the rim of a glass, cut six circles approximately the same size as the cakes. Set one circle atop each cake.

In a small saucepan, heat the remaining ⅓ cup coconut milk over medium-low heat until just bubbling, 1 to 2 minutes. Add the remaining ½ cup chocolate chips and cook, stirring, until blended and smooth, 2 minutes. Remove from the heat and cool for at least 10 minutes to thicken.

Smooth 1 tablespoon of the chocolate sauce over each cake. Sprinkle with the sliced almonds, then dust each cake with confectioners' sugar.

SALTED BUTTERSCOTCH PUDDING

SERVES 6

Pudding is the quintessential all-American after-school dessert. I always loved the idea of the pull-top butterscotch puddings you find in the supermarket, but I have to say my homemade version wins. By starting with a perfectly salty butterscotch sauce, you achieve a more sophisticated take on the original. Plus, you can make a batch ahead of time and pull it out of the fridge whenever treats are in order!

FOR THE SALTED BUTTER-SCOTCH SAUCE:

½ cup (1 stick) unsalted butter

1½ cups lightly packed light brown sugar

½ cup heavy cream

2 tablespoons pure vanilla extract

2½ teaspoons fine sea salt

½ teaspoon distilled white vinegar

FOR THE PUDDING:

3 cups whole milk

1½ cups heavy cream

6 egg yolks

7 tablespoons cornstarch

¼ teaspoon fine sea salt

1 tablespoon pure vanilla extract

Sweet Whipped Cream (page 68)

MAKE THE SAUCE:

In a medium saucepan, melt the butter over medium-high heat. Just before the butter has completely melted, add the brown sugar and stir with a wooden spoon until incorporated. Increase the heat to high, bring to a boil, then reduce the heat to medium and cook, stirring occasionally and making sure to stir around the edges of the saucepan, until the mixture first looks like grainy molten lava and then is completely smooth, 3 to 4 minutes. Whisk in the cream and cook until fully incorporated, 1 minute. Remove from the heat and whisk in the vanilla, salt, and vinegar.

MAKE THE PUDDING:

In a medium saucepan, whisk together the milk, cream, egg yolks, cornstarch, and salt until smooth. Set the pan over medium-high heat and cook, whisking continuously, until the mixture has thick-ened, 9 to 10 minutes. Strain the pudding through a fine-mesh sieve into a bowl, pushing it through with a silicone spatula or wooden spoon, then whisk in the vanilla. Slowly whisk the cooled butter-scotch sauce into the still-warm pudding base until fully incorporated. Cool for 10 minutes, then cover with plastic wrap, pressing it directly against the surface of the pudding to prevent a skin from forming, and chill until completely cold, at least 2 hours.

Divide the chilled pudding among six parfait cups or bowls and top with whipped cream.

STRAWBERRY FRUIT JEWELS

MAKES 64 JELLIES

Known as *pâtes de fruits* in France, where sweets shops arrange them like gems in a jewel box, these bright little squares are the essence of fruit. I chose strawberries, since you can find good organic ones practically year-round (of course, they're at their best in peak season). Since the method can be a little testy, this is a recipe that really calls for a candy thermometer; if you use one, they'll come out firm enough to cut and roll in sugar—and with that signature melt-in-your-mouth texture.

Cooking spray

5 cups fresh strawberries, hulled, rinsed, and dried

1½ tablespoons fresh lemon juice

2 cups sugar

3 tablespoons liquid pectin

Spray an 8-inch square baking pan with cooking spray, then line the bottom and sides of the pan with two strips of parchment paper that fit the pan both vertically and horizontally, leaving a 2-inch overhang on all sides. Spray the parchment with cooking spray.

In a food processor, process the strawberries until fully pureed, 30 seconds. Strain through a fine-mesh sieve into a heavy-bottomed small (2-quart) saucepan, discarding the seeds (you should have 2 cups puree), then add the lemon juice and ½ cup of the sugar.

Clip a candy thermometer to the side of the saucepan and bring the mixture to a boil over medium-high heat, stirring occasionally, until the temperature reaches 225°F. Reduce the heat to medium-low, slowly add the pectin and 1 cup of the sugar, and continue to stir the mixture until the temperature reduces to 200°F, 2 to 3 minutes. Increase the heat to medium and cook the mixture, stirring occasionally, until it reaches 225°F, thickens, coats the back of a spoon, and has the texture of honey or molasses, 5 minutes.

Remove from the heat and pour the mixture into the prepared pan, tipping to fill the corners and tapping the pan slightly to eliminate air bubbles. Cool to room temperature, at least 2 hours, until the candy springs back when pressed with your fingers and has a gel-like consistency (it should not be sticky). Use the parchment paper to lift the candy from the pan. Cut the candy into 1-inch squares with a greased paring knife. Pour the remaining ½ cup sugar into a shallow bowl. Working in batches, toss the squares in the sugar until fully coated. Serve immediately, or store in an airtight container in a cool place for up to 1 week.

CHEWY SEA SALT CARAMELS

MAKES 64 CARAMELS

You wouldn't be wrong to say I have a caramel obsession—the flavor shows up in different forms throughout this book. When sugar, cream, and butter cook together, they morph into a flavor that's universally loved—and super versatile. When you make caramel enough times, you start to learn that the fun is in how long you let it cook—the longer it goes, the deeper its color and flavor. Here, I take the caramel to the edge, in the process coaxing out as much complexity as possible before cutting and wrapping into individual candies. Just make sure that the darker the caramel gets, the more you're paying attention; those last few minutes are crucial!

Cooking spray

1 cup sweetened condensed milk

½ cup (1 stick) unsalted butter, cut into pieces

5 tablespoons heavy cream

½ cup light corn syrup

2 cups sugar

1½ tablespoons pure vanilla extract

1 teaspoon fine sea salt

1 teaspoon flaky sea salt, such as Maldon or fleur de sel, for sprinkling

64 (4-inch-square) cellophane candy wrappers or waxed paper wrappers

Spray an 8-inch square baking pan with cooking spray, then line the bottom and sides of the pan with two strips of parchment paper that fit the pan both vertically and horizontally, leaving a 2-inch overhang on all sides. Coat the parchment with cooking spray.

In a small saucepan, heat the condensed milk, butter, and cream over medium-low heat, whisking, until smooth and loose; remove from the heat. In a large (at least 4-quart) stainless-steel saucepan, combine the corn syrup and ½ cup water, then slowly pour the sugar into the center of the saucepan, being careful not to splash the sides of the pan (this helps avoid crystallization later). Give the mixture a gentle stir with a spatula and cook over medium-high heat, without stirring but swirling the saucepan occasionally, until the mixture turns a deep golden color, 13 to 17 minutes. Do not take your eyes off the saucepan, since the last stages of the caramelization happen very quickly!

Remove the saucepan from the heat and add the cream mixture; it will bubble up dramatically, then subside. Stir with a silicone spatula, then return to the stovetop over medium-low heat and simmer, stirring occasionally, until the mixture darkens and thickens, 4 to 7 minutes. Stir in the vanilla and fine sea salt, immediately pour the mixture into the prepared pan, cool for 5 minutes, then sprinkle with the flaky salt. Let rest at room temperature for 1 hour, then chill until the caramels firm up slightly, 1 hour more.

Use the parchment paper to lift the caramels out of the pan and set on a cutting board. Cut into 1-inch squares and place each caramel in a wrapper; twist the sides to seal.

AUNT KATHY'S CINNAMON ROLLS

MAKES 18 ROLLS

Every Christmas, Aunt Kathy makes batch upon batch of these gooey, cinnamon-scented, pull-apart rolls and gifts them to friends and family so they have something fresh and delicious to warm up and enjoy while unwrapping holiday gifts. The recipe was handed down from her mother, and I'm so honored she shared it with me here.

FOR THE DOUGH:

½ cup (1 stick) unsalted butter, plus more for greasing

1 cup whole milk

2 (¼-ounce) packages dry yeast (about 4½ teaspoons yeast)

½ cup sugar

1 teaspoon fine sea salt

5 cups bread flour

3 large eggs, at room temperature

FOR THE CINNAMON FILLING:

½ cup (1 stick) unsalted butter, softened

1 cup sugar

1 cup lightly packed light brown sugar

2 tablespoons ground cinnamon

3 to 4 tablespoons chopped pecans, raisins, or a combination of the two

FOR THE ICING:

½ cup (1 stick) unsalted butter, melted

2 cups confectioners' sugar, sifted

1 teaspoon pure vanilla extract

2 tablespoons whole milk, or more if necessary

MAKE THE DOUGH:

Grease a large ceramic or glass bowl with butter. In a small saucepan, heat the milk over medium-high heat, making sure it does not boil; when you see tiny bubbles form on the side of the pan, remove it from the heat. Stir in the butter and cool.

In a small bowl, combine the yeast, 1 tablespoon of the sugar, and 2 tablespoons tepid water, and set aside to bloom for 10 minutes.

In the bowl of a stand mixer fitted with the paddle attachment, beat the remaining sugar with the salt and the milk mixture on medium-low speed until incorporated, 1 minute. Add 2 cups of the flour and beat for 1 to 2 minutes more. Add the yeast mixture and beat for 1 minute more. Add the eggs one at a time, beating after each addition until incorporated. Stop the mixer and switch to the hook attachment. Add the remaining 3 cups flour and knead on

medium-high speed until the dough forms a smooth ball, 8 to 10 minutes (you can also knead by hand on a clean work surface). Transfer the dough to the prepared bowl, cover with plastic wrap followed by a clean kitchen towel, and place in a warm spot to rise for about 2 hours.

MAKE THE CINNAMON ROLLS:

Butter three 9-inch round cake pans. Whisk the sugars and cinnamon in a small bowl. After the dough has risen, place it on a lightly floured work surface and knead a few times with floured hands until the dough is no longer sticky. Divide it into three equal pieces. Using a rolling pin, roll out one piece into a thin 12-inch circle on a lightly floured work surface. Spread one-third of the softened butter evenly on top of the dough, followed by one-third each of the cinnamon-sugar mixture and the pecans and/or raisins. Roll the dough over the filling into a tube and cut it into six equal-size pieces. Place the pieces cut-side up in the prepared pan and set aside to rise again, covered loosely with plastic wrap or a clean kitchen towel, for 1 hour until almost doubled in size. Repeat with the remaining dough and filling.

Twenty minutes before baking, preheat the oven to 350°F. Bake the rolls until golden brown, 20 minutes. Cool slightly before icing.

MAKE THE ICING:

In the bowl of a stand mixer fitted with the paddle attachment, beat the butter, sugar, vanilla, and milk on low speed until just combined, then increase the speed to medium and beat until smooth, 1 minute. Spread the icing evenly over the still-warm buns.

RESOURCES

Making from-scratch desserts is one thing, and serving them is another thing altogether! Finding that perfect plate, tray, or dish to complement your creation takes a sweet experience to another level. I gravitate toward pieces that have an organic, handmade feel; they help reinforce the idea that you've made something special worth celebrating.

My friend designer Jenni Kayne (jennikayne.com) has the most beautiful pieces on her website, like pie plates and rolling pins by Farmhouse Pottery, as well as modern cake domes and cake servers.

Heath Ceramics (heathceramics.com) is known for its earthy yet polished pottery. They also sell gorgeous cutlery, cutting boards, and more.

Other great resources for serving pieces are March (marchsf.com), Garde (gardeshop.com), Food52 (food52 .com), and Aplat (aplatsf.com).

Quality bakeware is an investment well made; purchasing good pieces will ensure that the best ingredients are baked optimally. For KitchenAid mixers, baking cups and spoons, silicone spatulas, Pyrex mixing bowls, and even Cup4Cup gluten-free flour blend, I can always depend on Williams-Sonoma; in addition to their website (williamssonoma.com), they have stores in most major cities.

For the Chicago Metallic baking pans I can't live without (and pretty much any other kitchen gadget you could ever need), I turn to Sur La Table (surlatable.com).

Crate and Barrel has a great selection of Le Creuset baking dishes and OXO brand liquid measuring cups and other baking tools.

Amazon (amazon.com) is an easy place to find my favorite cocoa, Callebaut, and hard-to-find ingredients like maple sugar. For the best flour, you can't beat King Arthur (kingarthurflour.com).

Wilton (wilton.com) and Michaels (michaels.com) sell a large selection of cupcake liners, fondant (as well as fondant rollers and cutters), coloring gels, and the 12-cup pan called for in our cupcake recipes.

Cake rounds, as well as piping bags and tips, can be found online at gloriascakecandysuplys.com.

A great site for birthday candles (like the tall ones on page 270) is Knot and Bow (knotandbow.com). They can also be found at Anthropologie stores (anthropologie .com).

CopperGifts.com is my source for cookie cutters in every shape and size, as well as all type of cookie decorating supplies.

For Sprinkles offset spatulas, cupcake trays, and disposable cupcake towers, come into a Sprinkles store or find them online at sprinkles.com.

ACKNOWLEDGMENTS

To my boys, for always being delighted every time a new creation emerges from the oven. And thank you for your many new cupcake flavor ideas; they are a bit tricky to execute, but they are ingenious! Your sweet faces and kind hearts light up my world.

Mom, from your fabulous dinner party creations to the stories of your "Nana" Margaret, the restaurateur, from our trips to Paris to find the perfect meringue to the ones down the block to Swensen's for a sundae—thank you for instilling in me a love of baking and the pleasure of great food.

To Dad, for being our #1 Sprinkles cheerleader. But if you are going to wear your Sprinkles hat every single day, please let me give you a new one!!!

To Chuck and Lynda, my in-laws, for providing priceless counsel on Sprinkles strategy as well as making emergency runs to Smart and Final or the bank...and folding thousands of cupcake boxes! Thank you for being our support and on-the-ground PR team at all store openings. We would never have made so many friends on our own!

Adeena Sussman, my everything in this book! What a beautiful partnership! Thank you for your perfect prose and for shepherding me through the entire experience (and talking me off a few ledges!). Your talent and grace know no bounds.

Amy Neunsinger for your exquisite and singular vision for this book and for never being satisfied with what is expected. You are unstoppable!

Andy McNicol, for believing in a Candace beyond cupcakes and helping me envision and champion a book that reflects that. Thank you for steering me over the finish line.

Karen Murgolo, my editor at Grand Central, for patiently answering all my many, many, many questions about this process, as well as for your tireless editing and wonderfully positive notes in the manuscript sidelines. I really appreciated those!! Thank you also to your entire team: Ivy McFadden, Siri Silleck, Erin Vandeveer, Liz Connor, Amanda Pritzker, Nick Small, and Morgan Hedden, for their expert and reassuring guidance throughout this process. And a special thanks to Shubhani Sarkar for the book's beautiful design.

To Marcy Engelman, there are no words. You are simply the best at what you do. Thank you for your tireless passion for Sprinkles and for this book. Thank you for believing in my goals, and thank you for your friendship.

To my shoot team:

Frances Boswell, you are a genius in the kitchen. Your food is literally art. I'm so honored to have worked with you!

Kate Martindale, for making sure we always had the perfect accessory! You made every day a party.

Max Lesser, thank you for your incredible cooking and for keeping us nourished with your sensational Morning Glory nuts and brittles on set!

To my styling dream team: Andrew Zepeda, Georgie Eisdell, and Jessica DeRuiter. You make visual magic!

To all the Sprinkles employees who made the book and shoot possible:

Julie Masino, Stephen Snyder, Nicole Schwartz, Ellen Huggins, Dustin Scheerer, Jodi Moore, Alexia Moten, and our incredible team of bakers and frosters at Sprinkles Beverly Hills, including Mirian and Delmi.

And to my home team: Perla, Fita, and Lia. Thank you for braving the storm of the shoot with such calm!

To Julie Tanous, Holly Loring, Anat Abramov, Amy Tischler, Gayle Squires, and Sharon B. Oberfeld, who faithfully and patiently tested and retested—then retested again—the recipes in this book.

Thanks also to Tammy Haldeman, Kathy Rodgers, Neeley Snyder, Katie Michelle, Regan Elizabeth, Addison Grace, Chris Ramirez, Shayla Goins, Sharon Wieder, and Melissa Tran for your recipe testing help!

To Jane Buckingham, for being a constant source of encouragement to me (and so many women!) and for leading me to Andy. Your "do what I say I'm going to do" approach to life is my inspiration. This book would not exist without you.

To Richard Weitz, for your support at WME and for giving me the conviction to finally get this project off the ground. You make me feel like anything is possible.

To Sprinkles's exceptional employees, for going the extra mile in everything you do! And to Sprinkles's amazing customers, for celebrating your special moments with us.

My inimitable community of women friends...for your support and motivation throughout this very long process. Thank you for weighing in on recipes, concepts, outfits, and more...and for reminding me that "done is better than perfect." My life is very full because of you.

And finally, to Charles, my official recipe taster for over a decade and the best partner ever, in life and business.

INDEX

C

ABOUT THE AUTHOR

CANDACE NELSON is the founder and pastry chef of Sprinkles, the world's first cupcake bakery. Her ingredients-driven, sophisticated take on the classic American cupcake made Sprinkles an overnight bakery sensation and established Candace as a businesswoman to watch, as well as a pop culture icon featured everywhere from *Oprah*, *Vanity Fair*, and *People* magazines to *Good Morning America* and *The Martha Stewart Show*. Since the beginning, Candace's cupcakes, made from only the best ingredients and baked fresh throughout the day, have inspired long lines of devoted fans as well as accolades from the likes of Oprah Winfrey and Blake Lively.

Today, Sprinkles has over twenty locations nationwide and a growing number of Cupcake ATMs and Sprinkles Ice Cream shops selling all-American ice cream and cookie confections. Candace was a judge on the hit Food Network show *Cupcake Wars*, which filmed ten seasons, and airs around the world. A former investment banker, Candace is a graduate of Tante Marie's Professional Pastry Program in San Francisco and Wesleyan University.

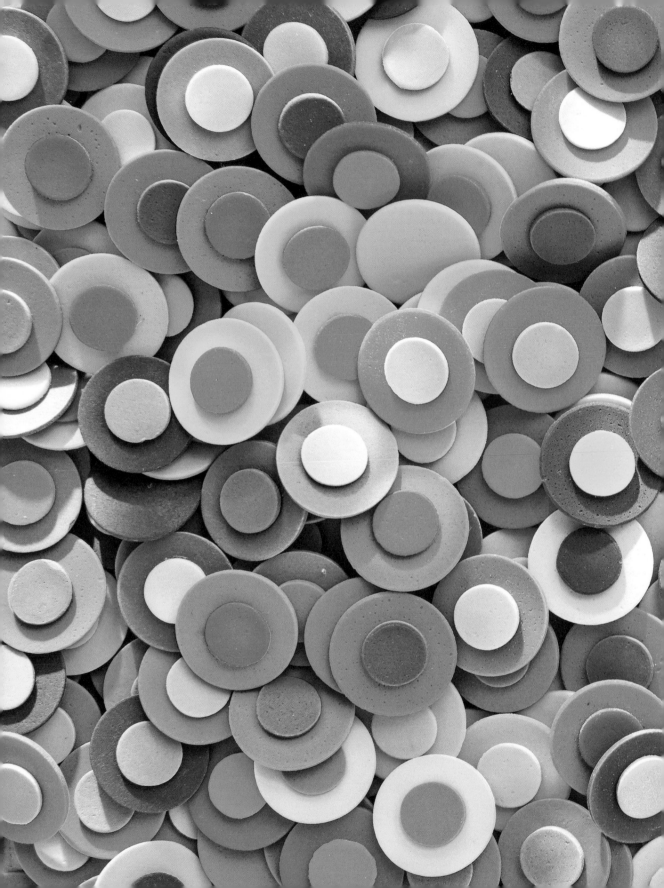